**VAMPIRE
STORIES**

Thirsty Hearts

W0235686

Julia Ross

Compact Verlag

© 2010 Compact Verlag GmbH München
Alle Rechte vorbehalten. Nachdruck, auch auszugsweise,
nur mit ausdrücklicher Genehmigung des Verlages gestattet.
Redaktion: Helga Aichele
Fachredaktion: Oliver Astley
Produktion: Wolfram Friedrich
Typographischer Entwurf: EKH Werbeagentur GbR, textum GmbH
Umschlaggestaltung: EKH Werbeagentur GbR
Titelabbildungen: www.Fotolia.com: Dmitrijs Dmitrijevs, Julien Gremillot,
Dmytro Tolokonov

ISBN 978-3-8174-7952-8
7279521

Besuchen Sie uns im Internet: www.compactverlag.de

Vorwort

Liebe Leserin, lieber Leser,

so packend war Englisch lernen noch nie! Diese Vampire Story kombiniert romantische Hochspannung mit dem bewährten didaktischen Konzept der Compact Lernlektüren.

Das vorliegende Buch wurde speziell für Lernende der Stufe B2 des Europäischen Referenzrahmens konzipiert. Vokabelerklärungen direkt auf der Seite erleichtern das Lesen. Jedes Kapitel wird durch abwechslungsreiche Übungen ergänzt, die auf unterhaltsame Weise Wortschatz, Textverständnis und Grammatik trainieren und festigen. Infokästen weisen auf sprachliche und grammatikalische Besonderheiten hin. Alle Vokabeln können Sie im Glossar noch einmal nachschlagen.

Viel Spaß und Erfolg
beim Englisch lernen mit Biss!

Inhalt

Zu diesem Buch

In einem kleinen schottischen Dorf rettet Luka die junge Alison, als sie von einem Verrückten angegriffen wird. Beide fühlen sich sofort zueinander hingezogen und kommen sich schnell näher – doch dann entdeckt Alison, dass Luka ein Vampir ist!
Völlig durcheinander kehrt Alison nach London zurück, doch sie kann die Nacht mit Luka nicht vergessen. Und auch Luka fühlt mehr für Alison als ihm lieb ist – mehr als er in Jahrhunderten gefühlt hat. Er folgt ihr nach London, aber dort lauern schon seine Feinde auf ihn. Als auch Alison in Gefahr gerät, muss Luka alles riskieren, um sie zu beschützen ...

1  After Nightfall

The wind **howled** all around the girl, her body a lonely silhouette against the sunset. It was winter, and night was falling faster than she had expected.

She pulled her warm coat tightly around her and walked further into the growing blackness. All around, the **barren** moorland was becoming dark and filled with strange shadows.

The girl was walking alone. She often made this journey along the road between two villages in the Scottish Highlands, where she had lived all of her life. She rarely met any other travellers on this road, and if she did, they were sure to be friends or relatives. There were few strangers in these parts. And yet she felt somehow unsure that she was alone tonight.

The howling of the wind through the weather-beaten landscape was **unsettling**, and the girl began to walk faster. She could feel the fear rising in her throat until the sound of her own deep and heavy breathing seemed louder than the wind.

Little sunlight remained, and there was no moon to light the empty night. She knew that there could be nobody else nearby, but turned to look behind her. There was nothing there but the

to howl	heulen
barren	karg, öde
unsettling	beunruhigend
dim	matt, schwach
desolate	trostlos

far-away lights of Fairburn. In the other direction, she could see the **dim** lights of the second village in the distance. The road towards them had never seemed longer or more **desolate**.

The girl continued walking, faster and faster, and slowly the lights grew nearer. The last of the sunlight had now left the sky, and there was a biting chill in the air. She could feel the cold in her bones.

The attack came without warning. The girl heard no sound, and did not see the figure that was hiding behind the dark, pointed rocks, waiting. All she saw was the blackness of the sky and the lights of her home – so close, but suddenly turning dark.

Her scream cut through the night for a moment, then disappeared into the wind.

chill	Kälte
pointed	spitz
to drown out	übertönen

Übung 1: Definitions. Ordnen Sie die Begriffe ihren Definitionen zu!

Highlands   chill   pointed   howl

1. Having a sharp end   _____

2. A cry like that of a dog or wolf   _____

3. An uncomfortable feeling of coldness   _____

4. The mountainous region of Scotland   _____

Alison Monroe shivered. It was a bitterly cold night and her grandmother's old cottage did little to keep out the Scottish chill.

Although Alison had grown up in Scotland, she had become used to warmer weather – or there was better central heating – since moving to London.

Pulling a blanket around her, Alison turned up the television to drown out the howling wind. Winter weather always seemed unfriendly to her, but the screams of the wind that night were unsettling her more than usual.

She turned back to the television screen. A silent film was *flickering* in black and white. Alison loved old horror movies. With the *fierce* wind beating down on the old stone cottage, it seemed like the perfect time to watch one of her favourite vampire films.

The old-fashioned music reached a crescendo: the *twisted* shadow of the vampire's hand was *creeping* across the pure white dress of the sleeping woman. A moment later, the woman awoke, sat *bolt upright* and opened her mouth in a silent scream. Then the vampire could be seen in full view. It had no hair on its head, its ears were pointed, and its fingers were long and twisted.

Alison almost wanted to laugh. How strange, she thought, that people found this creature frightening when the film was first seen! Now it seemed little more than ridiculous.

to flicker	flimmern, flackern
fierce	*hier:* stürmisch
twisted	verzerrt
to creep	kriechen
bolt upright	kerzengerade
to conclude	schließen, enden

Alison's grandmother, Eve, came into the room and sat down on the shabby sofa next to her granddaughter.

"I'll never understand how you can enjoy this type of thing, my dear!" Eve said.

"Silent films are beautiful," Alison explained. "Sometimes you can say more without using words, I think. Look at the way they use shadows in this scene... it's so atmospheric, you don't even need to see the vampire."

"Well, I'm glad they invented sound before I started going to the cinema, anyway," *concluded* Eve. "Let me have a look, there must be something better on another channel. Here we are, this looks good – he's ever so handsome, isn't he?"

The strange, pale vampire on the screen had disappeared. In its place was a tall man walking with a young woman through the gardens of a large house in the countryside. Alison recognized it as an adaptation of a well-known historical romance novel.

⚡ Och, aye!	Oh, ja! (schott.)
cloak	Umhang

"Shouldn't we start making dinner soon?" she asked, changing the subject. Eve looked at her watch.

"**Och, aye!** We probably should, dear. I'm not sure what we have in the fridge... could you check?"

Alison stood up, pulled the blanket around her shoulders like a woolly **cloak** and walked over to the fridge.

"There's some chicken, a couple of onions, some carrots that have seen better days... um, some milk... not much else. I should go to the shop now before it closes."

"Do you want me to take you in the car?" Eve asked.

"No, don't be silly. It's only a five-minute walk to the village store. I won't be long."

Übung 2: True or false? Kreuzen Sie die richtigen Aussagen an!

1. Alison is watching a brand new film. ❐

2. Eve wants to watch the vampire film with Alison. ❐

3. Alison will go to the shop to buy ingredients for dinner. ❐

4. Alison thinks the atmosphere is just right for watching a vampire film. ❐

Alison put on her warmest coat, picked up her purse and opened the door. Although she knew the night was cold, she was not prepared for the biting chill that greeted her. She grabbed a scarf on her way out and stepped into the black night.

She had only walked a few metres before she saw the village's only bus stop ahead. Buses did not come often, and never in the even-

solitary	einzeln
to slump	zusammensacken
bus shelter	Wartehäuschen
cautiously	vorsichtig
to dismiss	abtun, aufgeben

ing, so it surprised her to see a solitary figure waiting on the seat. Something about the way that the person was slumped, unmoving, made her feel very uneasy. She walked towards the bus shelter slowly and cautiously. Should she explain that there would be no bus that night? For a split second, a more irrational thought came into her mind: what would she do if the person was dead? She dismissed the ridiculous idea.

As Alison moved closer, though, there was still no movement from the seated figure. Its head hung unnaturally to the side and its clothes did not look warm enough for this bitter night.

Suddenly, Alison remembered that the local pub, The Old Banner, was just around the corner from the bus stop. The figure was probably one of her grandmother's neighbours who had had too much to drink and not made it home. She should wake him up and send him home to his bed.

Übung 3: Plural forms. Bilden Sie die Pluralformen der folgenden Substantive!

1. person   _____

2. scarf   _____

3. bus   _____

4. bus stop   _____

More confidently, Alison approached the man. It was clear from his slumped position that he had enjoyed too much alcohol. She laughed a little at herself for misinterpreting this simple scene and moved to wake him, smiling and **extending** her hand towards his shoulder. A friendly warning was all the man needed…

"Hey, you shou–"

Her words were cut short immediately. The stranger had grabbed her by the throat and was pulling her close with his other arm, bringing her face just centimetres away from his wild, wide-open eyes. His face was pale and **frenzied** and he was **growling** in an unnatural way. This was definitely no drunk.

to extend	ausstrecken
frenzied	wild, verzerrt
to growl	knurren
choked	erstickt
hiss	Fauchen
to expose	freilegen, zeigen
fang	Reißzahn, Vampirzahn
dagger	Dolch

The incredible speed and focus of the attack gave Alison no time to think. She could not even scream. Instinct alone made her push against the stranger with all of her weight, trying to get free of his grip, but his strength seemed almost superhuman.

"What do you want?" she cried out. Her voice came out **choked** and shrill.

Her attacker did not reply, but simply stared at her coldly with a half-smile flickering on his thin lips. Then, terrifyingly, he let out a cat-like **hiss** which **exposed** teeth that looked very much like **fangs**. They shone like **daggers** in the dim yellow light. While pulling her closer still, he opened his mouth and brought his pointed teeth towards her neck.

Alison tried with all her strength to push him away, but everything was happening too fast. She was struggling as hard as she could, but his steely grip made her attempts seem weak and useless. She could not hope to match his power.

Only her scarf now stood between her neck and the deadly fangs of the inhuman creature that had **trapped** her. She could not believe what was happening: surely she could not die tonight, not like this!

Übung 4: Fill in the blanks. Ergänzen Sie die fehlenden Wörter!

1. The stranger *g*_____ Alison by the throat.

2. The inhuman creature's *f*_____ were getting closer

and closer to Alison's *n*_____ .

3. The *a*_____ was incredibly fast and focused.

4. Only Alison's *s*_____ was protecting her from a

deadly *b*_____ .

Alison suddenly felt herself being pulled away from her attacker. Something had grabbed her from behind and pulled her out of the way very fast, though she did not feel any pain. Momentarily, she thought she **glimpsed** a second pair of fangs out of the corner of her eye as she fell to the ground. She could see now that a second man had joined the violent scene; he was fighting the creature with forceful **blows**.

Alison did not want to stay to find out who, or what, this second stranger was, but fear and shock kept her **glued to the spot**. In front

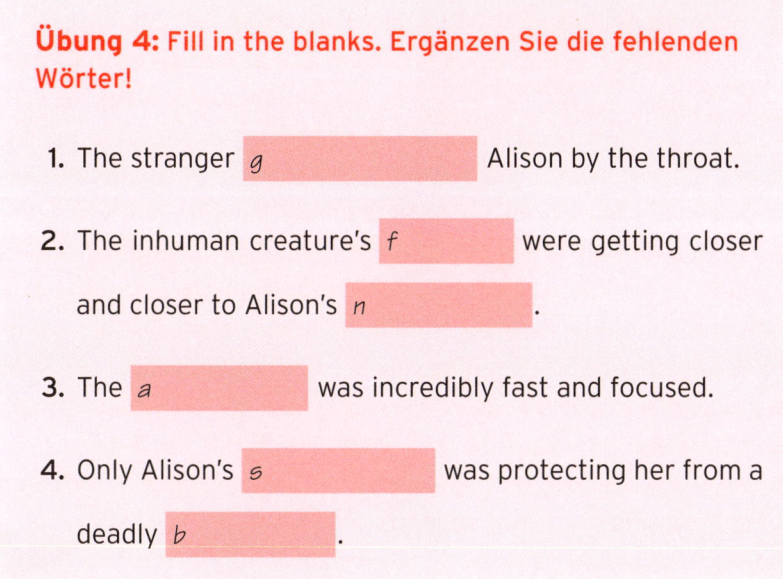

to trap	in eine Falle locken, fangen
to glimpse	flüchtig erblicken
blow	Schlag, Hieb
to be glued to the spot	wie angewurzelt dastehen

of her she saw the fight continue, but in her panic she could not make out what was happening. Desperately, Alison tried to turn around, get up and run to safety. She was **gasping** for air and could hear the desperation of her short, loud breathing.

To make out bedeutet hier „verstehen, schlau werden aus", kann aber auch „ausmachen, er-kennen" oder „entziffern" bedeuten.

Finally, she managed to stand. But as soon as she began to move, she felt a hand on her back and quickly turned to hit it away. At last she found the power to scream. A raw, animal sound **burst from** her and she raised her arms, ready to fight. But to her surprise, there was now only one man behind her, and it was not her attacker. He had moved outside of the shelter, and in the light she could now see clearly that he was human, like her – she must have imagined the fangs in her shock and confusion. The man's face seemed kind, and he was standing a little way away with his hands in the air to show that he did not want to hurt her.

Alison slumped back on the floor, feeling her neck for blood. She was not injured, and she **sensed** that the horror had passed.

"Was that a…"

"…vampire?" the man cut in. "No. The man who attacked you is a madman, but he's no vampire."

His voice was low and gentle, but the slight **hint** of a foreign accent gave it a harder sound.

"But the fangs…," Alison began.

"**Fake**," the man said. "It's some kind of **obsession** he has. It seems

to gasp	keuchen, nach Luft schnappen
to burst from	herausbrechen aus
to sense	spüren, wahr-nehmen
hint	*hier:* Andeutung, Hauch
fake	unecht
obsession	Manie, Besessen-heit
to prey on	Jagd machen auf

he likes to **prey on** young girls – another woman was attacked just an hour ago between here and Fairburn. Are you hurt?"

"No, I don't think so," Alison said, feeling her neck again.

Übung 5: Adverbs. Lesen Sie weiter und ergänzen Sie die Adverbien!

Alison's fear **1.** slow _____ began to leave her.

Still breathing **2.** heavy _____, she closed her

eyes for a moment and breathed **3.** deep _____.

The man **4.** gentle _____ put his hand on her

shoulder as if to tell her that everything was all right.

Within a few moments she was feeling calmer, but her heart

was still beating **5.** wild _____ in her chest.

Alison stood back to try to take in the situation. It was true that the attack had seemed somehow unreal to her, and she was grateful for this stranger's logical explanation. Her own ideas seemed rather foolish now: of course there was no such thing as vampires!

The man did not look like he was going to speak again. He had a stern look that made him seem distant and a little cold. Nevertheless, Alison was determined to find out more.

stern	streng, hart
distant	*hier:* unnahbar
to shudder	schaudern, frösteln

"How did he move so... so unnaturally? He was so fast and strong – I couldn't do anything to stop him!"

"I imagine most attacks must seem that way to the victim. You must have been in a lot of shock. He's a very violent and dangerous man... I'm sorry that I didn't find you sooner."

"I'm glad you found me at all!"

Alison shuddered at the thought of what could have happened if her strange rescuer had not appeared on the scene.

Übung 6: Vocabulary quiz. Finden Sie die beschriebenen Begriffe und enträtseln Sie das Lösungswort!

1. A sound of terror   S C _ _ _ ☐

2. A blood-sucking creature   _ _ _ _ ☐R _

3. The man looked stern and   ☐_ _ T _ _ _

4. The opposite of a smile   _ R _ _ ☐

5. The attacker was very   _ ☐_ L _ _ _ _

6. Risky or unsafe   _ _ _ ☐_ R _ U _

7. To shake because you are frightened   _ ☐_ D _ _ _

8. What the police do when they catch a criminal   _ R _ _ _ ☐

Lösung: ☐☐☐☐☐☐☐☐

"Where did he disappear to so fast?" Alison asked.

"He ran away into the moors before I could hold him down. I hoped I would be able to catch him and hand him in to the police, but he got away."

"Should we call the police now, do you think?" she asked, surprised that this thought had not occurred to her sooner.

"They're already waiting at his house to arrest him, and there are men like me all around the area watching out to make sure that he doesn't attack again. You should tell the police about what happened later on, but for now let's just get you home safely."

Alison stood up, but she was feeling so **shaken** that it was difficult to **support herself**. Fortunately, the man put his arm around her and helped her walk slowly back towards the cottage. "I'm Luka, by the way," he said. Alison's shock was beginning to

shaken	erschüttert, aufgewühlt
to support oneself	*hier:* sich auf den Beinen halten
to fade	nachlassen, verblassen
rugged features *pl*	markante Gesichtszüge
captivating	fesselnd, eindringlich
tentative	zaghaft, zögerlich

fade. She looked at Luka for a few moments, taking in his appearance for the first time. Now was not the time to notice such things, but she could not help but see that he was very handsome. His dark hair and **rugged features** were an attractive contrast to his pale skin, and in this low light his strangely **captivating** eyes seemed almost completely black. His obvious physical strength made her feel safe in the darkness.

Übung 7: Unscramble the dialogue. Lesen Sie weiter, indem Sie die folgenden Sätze chronologisch ordnen!

a) "You don't need to thank me," Luka told her with a **tentative** smile.

b) "Ever since I heard about the first attack."

c) "I'm Alison. I suppose I should thank you for saving me."

d) "Have you been out here long?"

e) "You must be cold," Alison said stupidly, reaching out to touch Luka's hand. As she had guessed, it felt almost frozen.

1	2	3	4	5

to wash over sb.	jmd. überkommen
exhaustion	Erschöpfung
gradually	allmählich, nach und nach
to regain consciousness	wieder zu Bewusstsein kommen
blank	leer

They soon reached the gate of her grandmother's house, and, to her surprise, Alison found herself wishing that the walk had taken longer.

"Will you come in?" she asked. "You could stay for a while and help me explain to my grandma what happened."

But Luka shook his head.

"I should go back to keeping watch over this road. I won't sleep tonight until that madman is caught."

"You're right. But perhaps we could meet up tomorrow, or later on. I haven't thanked you properly yet."

There was something about this man that excited her curiosity[i].

"There's no need," Luka replied, looking deeply into her eyes.

Disappointed, Alison opened her mouth to speak again, but suddenly a very strange feeling washed over her. She was struggling to keep her eyes open. Perhaps it was exhaustion after the adrenaline and emotion of the last few minutes. Everything around her was becoming unclear and fading into nothingness. The only thing that she could focus on was Luka's black eyes; the rest of the scene was gradually slipping away…

Curiosity bedeutet zumeist Neugier, kann aber auch Kuriosität bedeuten:
The museum is full of curiosities.

Through the fog in her mind, Alison heard the shrill sound of a woman's voice.

"Alie! Wake up! Please, Alie!"

Alison was slowly regaining consciousness. She opened her eyes and realized that the frightened, grey-haired woman in front of her was her grandmother.

Übung 8: Simple past. Lesen Sie weiter und setzen Sie die Verben ins Simple Past!

"Och, you had me scared!" Eve **1. exclaim** _____, a little calmer now.

She **2. put** _____ her arms around her granddaughter and **3. hold** _____ her tight.

"Are you all right, dear?"

Groggily, Alison **4. check** _____ that she **5. can** _____ move her arms and legs, fingers and toes.

"I'm fine, I think," she replied. "Why?"

"Well, I answered the doorbell, and there you were on the floor, unconscious! I brought you inside but you wouldn't wake up. Thank goodness you're all right. What on earth happened to you out there?"

Alison thought long and hard, but there was an empty space where the memory should be. She tried again and again to bring back anything from the last half an hour, but her mind was blank.

"I... I have no idea. I remember walking out the door, but then... nothing."

She was beginning to feel frightened. Nothing like this had ever happened to her before. Why had she passed out? Why couldn't she remember what had happened?

"You must have collapsed by the door," Eve guessed. "But who would have found you, rung the doorbell, and then left without waiting for me to open the door?"

There were no answers.

Alison shivered, feeling completely out of control.

"This is scary. I don't understand what's going on here..."

"Oh, you poor, dear thing," Eve responded. "We'll have to make sure you see a doctor tomorrow, but I think it's best for now to forget about dinner and get you into bed."

Alison did not disagree. She went with Eve to the small bedroom at the back of the house, where her bed had been made up with several warm blankets. It was still early, but the blackout had left her with a deep feeling of exhaustion. She longed to lose herself once again in the comfort of sleep.

Alison climbed into bed and let her grandmother pull the blankets over her. Outside, it was beginning to rain.

Übung 9: Odd one out. Welches Wort ist das „schwarze Schaf"? Markieren Sie das nicht in die Reihe passende Wort!

1. collapse   pass out   control   blackout

2. memory   empty   blank   vacant

3. amazing   incredible   dreadful   fantastic

4. exhausted   bolt upright   yawning   sleepy

Thunder cracked in the sky and a flash of lightning ripped through the darkness, bathing the room where Alison lay sleeping in a sudden light. As more thunder loudly fractured the night sky, she began to toss and turn in her bed.

There was another loud crack of thunder and Alison suddenly sat bolt upright. Rain was beating down heavily on the roof.

The frightening images of her nightmare still felt close. Was she really awake? The dream had seemed so real that it took her a moment to break free from her terror and realize, with relief, that it had all been in her head. She was safe in her bed.

And yet she still saw the fangs in her mind's eye. An attack, a hiss, a sleeping stranger… everything was coming back to her with a startling realism.

It must have been a bad dream, she knew that, but it didn't feel like one…

Slowly more details returned. She saw the face of a man, her rescuer.

to long	sich sehnen
to crack	*hier:* krachen
to rip	(zer)reißen
to fracture	(durch)brechen
to toss and turn	sich hin und her wälzen
startling	erschreckend, verblüffend
to drain	weichen, ab-fließen
clamouring	Toben

She heard his voice and saw him leading her through desolate moorland… then there were only his eyes… and then nothing but darkness.

Alison breathed in sharply. She felt as if the blood was draining from her, and the room began to spin: it had not been a dream. These were memories, she thought.

She recognized the scenery and remembered some of the events of the evening. She had left the house to go to the store and had been found unconscious by the door. But what had happened before…?

The stormy night outside continued its loud clamouring. Still Alison sat there, not wanting to move. She tried to convince herself that it was just the blackout, combined with the storm and the vampire film, that had put these fearful thoughts in her mind. That must be it. But the images remained so clear, particularly the face of the man, and the start of a name: Lu… Luke? Luka! She was certain. But who would have a name like that in a small Scottish village?

Übung 10: Fill in the blanks. Lesen Sie weiter und ergänzen Sie die fehlenden Wörter!

continued   pillow   sense   before   confused   echo

Alison felt **1.** _____ and frightened. There were hundreds of thoughts running through her mind at once and nothing seemed to help her make **2.** _____ of them. She pulled her **3.** _____ over her head of dark curls and tried to shut out her thoughts, but that name still seemed to **4.** _____ through her head: Luka, Luka, Luka...

Meanwhile the rain **5.** _____ to fall, playing percussion on the roof of the house. It would be a long time **6.** _____ she slept that night.

2  Reality Bites

A tiny orange **sliver** of the sun burst out of the darkness and began to climb the horizon. Morning was arriving, and night's shadows were beginning to disappear as light spread across the sky. Soon Alison would wake, but for now she lay peacefully sleeping.

The room was bathed in sunshine by the time Alison rolled over in bed, stretched her arms out above her head and opened her eyes. In the bright morning light, the horror of the night seemed long gone. It took some time for reality and dreams to begin to separate in her mind. Yesterday's events were gradually returning to her with a strange **cinematic** quality that made her feel more like a **spectator** than the protagonist. In the **faint** warmth of the winter sun, it was hard to believe that any of it had ever really happened at all.

sliver	*hier:* Schimmer, Strahl
cinematic	Kino-
spectator	Zuschauer
faint	schwach
vivid	lebhaft, lebendig

Her nightmare, with its absurd vampire attack, now seemed ridiculous to her. But how **vivid** it had all been at the time…

Putting her thoughts aside, Alison pulled back the blankets and got out of bed. One thing was for sure: she had passed out and should see a doctor as soon as possible.

She opened the kitchen door and found her grandmother already making tea. Two mugs were waiting on the table. Eve looked up immediately and hurried over to where Alison stood in the doorway.

"How are you feeling this morning, dear?" she asked in a kind voice.

"Absolutely fine, but I still feel confused about yesterday evening."
Alison rubbed her head and let her long dark hair fall messily over her shoulders.

"Nothing like that has ever happened to me before," she continued.
"I've never even fainted."

"It must be a horrible feeling, not remembering what happened,"
Eve said.

"Well, that's not completely new for me, Grandma," Alison joked, "but I would normally expect alcohol to be involved somewhere! Anyway, shall I call the doctor?"

"I already have. You've got an appointment at one o'clock – it was the earliest I could get."

"That's great. Thank you."

to faint	ohnmächtig werden
⚡ fellow	*hier:* Kerl, Typ
to blur	verschwimmen, undeutlich werden
night shift	Nachtschicht
to shed light on sth.	Aufschluss geben über etw.

Alison hugged Eve, and for a moment she lost herself and forgot her worries in the comforting familiarity of her grandmother's arms.

"Grandma…," she continued, "this is going to sound like a strange question, but is there someone called Luka in the village?"

"Let me see, Luka… yes, that sounds about right. There's a foreign fellow who lives right next to The Old Banner… I think that's his name. Something like that, anyway."

Alison shivered a little. The line that she had drawn between reality and dreams was suddenly blurred.

"Does he have dark hair?" she asked tentatively.

"Yes, that's right. A similar colour to yours. I really don't see him all that often, though. I think he works night shifts over in Inverness, or at least that's what I've heard. He keeps himself to himself, you see."

Alison wondered for a moment whether she should tell Eve about her nightmare, but it all still felt so unclear, confusing and frightening. She did not want to think any more about it until she had regained her own sense of reality.

"Why do you ask?" Eve asked with a raised eyebrow.

"Oh, no reason… I just heard the name and thought it sounded unusual. No reason at all."

Übung 11: Synonyms. Welche Begriffe haben dieselbe Bedeutung? Ordnen Sie zu!

1. ☐ vivid   **a)** viewer

2. ☐ hug   **b)** cautiously

3. ☐ faint   **c)** lifelike

4. ☐ tentatively   **d)** embrace

5. ☐ spectator   **e)** dim

The hospital visit took them longer than expected, and it **shed** frustratingly little **light on** Alison's blackout. After various tests, questions and examinations, the doctor announced that he could not find anything wrong with her. He suggested doing further tests, but Alison was not going to be staying in Scotland for long enough to have them[i]: she would be back in London

> **Have them** ist hier die Verkürzung von **to have the tests done** (sich den Untersuchungen unterziehen).

soon. Leaving the hospital, both women felt frustrated that they were no closer to knowing why Alison had fallen unconscious so suddenly, or whether it would happen again.

The hospital was some way away, and the journey back across the moors gave Alison time to think. She felt more and more certain that at least some of the answers to her questions lay with this mysterious Luka character. She believed that she would recognize his face, but had no waking memory of ever meeting him. And the whole thing still seemed so far-fetched that she could not truly bring herself to trust her own thoughts. But if, somehow, he was really the rescuer in her nightmare, then perhaps other details were also real – and maybe he would be able to explain them.

Eve drove in silence with a look of concern on her face. Alison still wondered whether she should tell her about the nightmare, but she did not want to add to her grandmother's worries. The dream did seem to offer clues to what had really happened, but they were mixed with other details that must surely be imaginary. Scaring Eve with vampire stories would not help anyone.

When they arrived home, Alison soon felt restless.

"Do you mind if I go and visit Jenny?" she asked almost as soon as they had walked through the door.

Jenny was a childhood friend who Alison often visited when she was in the village; she even stayed overnight on occasion. Alison did not expect there to be a problem with her request.

"Don't you think you should stay at home this evening, dear? Just in case you black out again?"

waking memory	bewusste Erinnerung
far-fetched	weit hergeholt, an den Haaren herbeigezogen
imaginary	eingebildet, erfunden
stunted	*hier:* knorrig
unobtrusive	unauffällig
tucked away	versteckt
to cling to sth.	sich (fest)klammern an
camouflage	Tarnbemalung

"But I've barely seen Jenny on this visit," Alison argued, "and she only lives a few minutes away. Please, it's important."

"After last night, I would be happier if you didn't, but I suppose it's your decision. Shall I at least walk you there?" Eve asked.

"Gran, I'll be fine! I can't live the **1.** Rest _____

of my life missing out on things just because I *might* have an-

other **2.** Ohnmacht _____. And the doctor

said he couldn't find anything wrong with me, anyway."

3. Mit diesen Worten _____, Alison

considered the discussion over. She put on her warm

winter **4.** Mantel _____ and scarf,

and **5.** öffnete _____ the door.

Alison stepped out into the cold afternoon and walked up towards The Old Banner. Her path was flanked by dark rocks and stunted, weather-beaten trees. She passed the village's only bus stop: empty as usual, she thought to herself.

It was a short walk to the pub, and soon enough she found herself beside the house that she was looking for. Oddly, she had never really noticed it before. It was not the size of the house that made it so unobtrusive, since it was not unusually small. It was more to do with its position, tucked away behind the pub as though hiding from view. Even the dark colour of the stone walls seemed to sink into the background, and plants clung to its rough surface like living camouflage. Alison felt slightly guilty for lying to her grandmother about where she was going. However, she felt that she had to solve this puzzle without Eve's help. Nobody would be able to understand why she saw fangs in her mind's eye or help her to make sense of her faint memories. Nobody, except perhaps Luka.

She rang the doorbell cautiously. A sense of unease was gradually choking her curiosity. While she waited for the door to open, she was beginning to think that it would be a relief if no one was home. But relief did not come. The door swung open and behind it she saw, in the raw clarity of daylight, the same face that she had seen so clearly in her dream. She felt a shock of recognition as her eyes met his.

Übung 13: Verb forms. Ergänzen Sie die Vergangenheitsformen der folgenden Verben!

1. feel _____ _____

2. hide _____ _____

3. ring _____ _____

4. cling _____ _____

5. relieve _____ _____

"Er... hi," Alison began clumsily. "I'm sorry to bother you, but are you Luka?"

"Yes, that's me."

His voice contained both hardness and a softer, gentle quality, Alison noticed. A slight foreign accent, somewhat Slavic, added to its unusual melody.

"Did we meet last night?" she asked tentatively.

"No," came the cold reply. "I'm afraid I can't help you."

With these few words, Luka moved to shut the door. However, to the surprise of both of them, a foot was blocking it, caught vulnerably between the inside and the outside of the house. Alison had placed it in the way of the closing door instinctively.

"I'm not leaving," she said with more courage than she felt. "I need to know what happened."

Luka looked down at the foot, then up at the determined face before him.

"You'd better come in," he finally said.

clumsily	ungeschickt, unbeholfen
Slavic	slawisch
vulnerably	verletzbar, prekär
insanity	Irrsinn
thud	dumpfer Schlag

Alison's unease grew as she entered the house, and suddenly she was hit by the insanity of the situation: here she was, allowing herself to be alone in the house of a stranger whom she had no reason to trust. But she knew that Luka was the only person who could shed some light on those mysterious missing minutes of the previous night. In the end, she was more curious than afraid. The door closed behind her with a thud.

Übung 14: Word search. Finden Sie im Suchrätsel acht Begriffe aus dem Text!

C	S	T	R	A	N	G	E	R
A	X	K	I	Q	C	D	E	J
F	W	U	N	E	A	S	E	Y
A	A	B	S	I	K	V	X	A
N	T	L	A	S	B	I	P	C
G	T	R	N	B	I	C	H	C
S	A	B	I	T	E	T	R	E
Z	C	W	T	G	R	I	L	N
F	K	A	Y	N	O	M	M	T

There was nothing unusual about the inside of the house that Alison could **put her finger on**. Perhaps it was her own feelings that made the everyday interior seem a little dark and threatening. Luka led Alison through the shabby hall into a rather old-fashioned living room.

The thick, heavy curtains were closed, even though it was not yet dark. There was a large central fireplace and wooden furniture lining most of the walls. On rows of shelves and on top of most of the furniture, there were more books than Alison had ever seen outside of a library.

Suddenly her examination of the house was interrupted by a stern voice.

"How did you find out where I live?"

Luka sounded angry, and his face was serious.

"My grandma told...," Alison began, but then a thought occured to her. "Hang on a moment, shouldn't I be the one asking the questions? You did meet me last night, so why did you say you didn't?"

Luka's expression suddenly changed to regret. He gestured for her to sit down, and she instinctively chose the seat furthest away from him.

"I'm sorry, Alison," he said in a nearly expressionless voice.

It surprised her only momentarily that he knew her name.

to put one's finger on sth.	etw. genau ausmachen
stab	Anflug, Stich

"You're right – we did meet last night," he continued. "I rescued you when you were attacked just a few hundred metres away from here. But then, as I was walking you back home, you collapsed. I didn't know what to do... I panicked."

"So you just *left* me by the door?"

Alison still felt a **stab** of anger at the thought of her poor grandmother finding her passed out outside. She knew how much it had frightened her.

"Yes, I carried you to the door and rang the doorbell, then I waited to make sure that someone found you. It was stupid of me, but at the time I thought that if I appeared on the doorstep with you unconscious, your grandma would think that I had hurt you. She might have been afraid of me, and all I wanted was for you to get home safe."

maniac	Verrückter
to flash	zucken, blitzen
rapidly	schnell
to suppress sth.	etw. verdrängen

Thoughts were clamouring inside Alison's head. "So, the attack... that was real?"

"Yes, you were attacked. Do you remember all of this?"

"I remember," Alison's voice trembled, "a... a vampire attacking me. But that's impossible!"

Luka put his large, strong hands on her shoulders and looked into her eyes. "I explained to you last night that the man who attacked you was..."

"A maniac," Alison cut in 🛈 as though speaking the words involuntarily. "With an obsession for vampires... I remember now! It's so strange, everything seems to be flooding back."

She closed her eyes and the missing scenes flashed rapidly through her consciousness like a horror film on fast forward.

"It's natural that your mind would suppress what happened," Luka

Phrasal Verbs mit **cut**
Es gibt zahlreiche Phrasal Verbs mit to cut. Hier einige Beispiele:

to cut in	unterbrechen, einwerfen
to cut away	wegschneiden
to cut back	stutzen, kürzen
to cut down	einschränken, kürzen
to cut off	abschneiden, unterbinden

explained calmly. "It must have been absolutely terrifying for you. Why don't you make yourself comfortable? I'll get you a drink."

Übung 15: Choose the correct word. Lesen Sie weiter und unterstreichen Sie die richtige Variante!

Alison thought that it would be difficult to get comfortable on such a hard **1.** armchair / wardrobe , but she accepted Luka's **2.** request / offer of a drink. While he was gone, she held her head in her hands and tried to make sense of her thoughts. Her **3.** beliefs / feelings towards Luka were changing. He was unusual, that was for sure, but there was something strangely **4.** captivating / tedious about him. Perhaps she would move onto the sofa so that she was a little closer to him when he **5.** returned / departed . She sat down on what looked like the most **6.** comfortable / enjoyable part of the sofa, but realized with a slight bump that it was hard, too.

Luka soon returned and handed her a drink.
"I hope you aren't still angry with me," he said with a half-smile.
"No, not at all," Alison replied honestly.
He had saved her, and she was grateful. She remembered now how Luka had bravely fought off her attacker, and how he had been determined not to rest until the man was found. That reminded her: "Did the police catch that maniac?"

"Yes, they did," Luka replied. "You don't need to worry; he'll be locked away for a long time."

Alison sighed with relief. Looking up into Luka's near-black eyes and ruggedly handsome face, she no longer felt scared, but protected. His **checked** shirt was thin enough for her to see the outline of the muscles below, and open just enough for a hint of chest hair to show at the top.

"Thank you, for everything," she said.

"I'm just sorry I didn't catch the man before he attacked you," Luka responded.

"Then we would never have met."

Alison felt herself becoming braver. She had a sudden desire to touch his broad chest and feel his strong arms around her.

Luka changed the subject. "Tell me about yourself, Alison. You don't speak with the same accent as most other people in the village. Perhaps I'm not the only one who doesn't quite belong here?"

Alison smiled. "No, you're right. My parents moved down south to England when I was a child, and now I only come here to visit my grandma and one or two old friends. What about you – what brought you to such a **remote** place? Where do you come from?"

| checked | kariert |
| remote | abgelegen |

"An even more remote place, if you can believe it. I come from a village in Serbia, high in the mountains."

"And is it even smaller than this village?" Alison asked curiously.

"Oh yes. This place beats my hometown by about twenty houses and a bus stop!"

"You must have been practically the only person there!" Alison joked. "Do you ever miss it?"

A dark shadow seemed to pass over Luka's expression.

"No," he replied, "not really."

1. A violently mad person _____

2. The place that you originally
   come from _____

3. Isolated, far away from
   civilization _____

4. A pattern of squares, often
   used in clothing _____

Outside, the sun was already setting. Even though Alison had not
taken off her coat, she could feel that there was a chill was in the air.
Luka turned away, then looked back towards Alison, whose cheeks
were glowing a pale pink.

"You look cold," he said. "I'll make a fire."

He stood up, **gathered** some wood and newspaper from a basket in
the corner and began placing them in
the fireplace. He knelt with his back
turned to Alison as he prepared the
fire, and soon her curiosity began to
get the better of her.

After a moment, she stood up from
the sofa and began to explore the

to gather sth.	etw. zusammen-suchen
to get the better of sb.	mit jmd. durchgehen
stack	Stapel
canvas	Leinwand

room. She saw a **stack** of **canvases** leaning against a wall, and began
to turn them over and look through them.

Luka turned around sharply from the fireplace, where golden orange flames now blazed in a violent frenzy of light. The fire's reflection flashed through his eyes, giving an impression of anger.

"Did you do these? They're incredible," Alison asked nervously, pointing at some paintings of the moorland by night.

"Don't touch those!" he ordered roughly.

"Oh… I'm sorry," she said in a small voice. "I didn't mean to be nosy."

"That's all right," Luka responded, softening. "I just don't like it when people look through my things without asking."

"If I had your talent I would be proud," she suggested quietly. "You did paint these, then?"

"That's right," he answered. "Look, I'm sorry for shouting at you. I guess I'm not too used to having visitors."

to blaze	(auf)lodern
frenzy of light	*hier:* Flammenspiel
in a small voice	mit leiser Stimme
nosy	neugierig
to sympathize	Mitleid haben, mit- fühlen
tight-knit community	enge Gemeinschaft

Alison sympathized. It must be difficult being the outsider in such a small, tight-knit community. She returned to the sofa, where Luka was now sitting.

"What do you do for a living around here anyway?"

"I work night shifts in a hospital in Inverness. I have the night off tonight, though," he replied.

"Are you a doctor?"

Luka laughed his rough, deep laugh. "No – I'm a cleaner!"

"What? Why?!" asked Alison impolitely. "I mean, you're so talented," she quickly added, "why don't you become an artist?"

"There isn't much demand for artists around here," Luka replied.

Alison sensed that he did not want to speak any more about the subject, but there were so many things she wanted to know. The muscular, handsome man sitting beside her was little more than a stranger, yet she was **intrigued** by the mysteries that seemed to make up his life story.

"Where did you learn to paint?" she eventually asked.

"I taught myself. But enough about me, what do you do?"

intrigued	fasziniert
telesales	Telefonmarketing
piercing	durchdringend, stechend
to hold sb. spellbound	jmd. in seinen Bann ziehen
carnal	körperlich, sinnlich
intimate	intim, vertraulich

"Nothing interesting," she said as she twisted her dark hair around one of her fingers. "I work in **telesales** for a big company in London. It's awful, but it pays the rent."

"So when are you returning to London?"

"Tomorrow."

She felt suddenly regretful that she could not stay longer. Something about Luka's **piercing** black eyes seemed to **hold her spellbound**. When he looked at her, her skin felt hot.

Übung 17: Characterisation. Ordnen Sie den beiden Personen die passenden Beschreibungen zu!

1. Alison: ☐☐☐   2. Luka: ☐☐☐

a) artistic

b) curious

c) speaks roughly

d) intriguing

e) glowing cheeks

f) works in telesales

The temperature in the room was rising, and Alison could feel the hot breath of the flames on her face. She was becoming warm, so she removed her coat and scarf. With a sudden, **carnal** shock, she felt the soft touch of Luka's hand on her neck. It was an **intimate** gesture, and Alison immediately felt her heartbeat quicken with desire.

"You weren't injured at all last night, were you?" he asked her as he ran his fingers slowly, sensually across her throat to feel for any slight injury.

"No, I don't think so..."

She knew for sure that she was not hurt, but the gentle tickle of Luka's fingers against her skin was too pleasurable to refuse. Involuntarily, she raised her head a little, exposing more of her pale neck.

Luka pulled his hand away and brought it back to rest on his thigh. But Alison was not so shy.

"Don't you ever get lonely here, without any visitors?" she asked invitingly.

Her hand had joined his, and her body now pressed lightly against his side.

Luka did not need to answer. Suddenly, and with a fierce passion, he lunged forward, took her face between both hands and kissed her hard on the lips. His hands were moving now, down to her shoulders, her arms and waist. She responded with a moan of lust and wrapped her arms around his shoulders, gently biting his lips.

Their two bodies writhed in unison and their mouths met hungrily. Luka's searching hands pulled at Alison's clothes, while hers reached under his shirt to feel the masculine contours of his chest.

sensually	sinnlich
tickle	Kitzel
involuntarily	unwillkürlich
thigh	Oberschenkel
to lunge	vorpreschen, stürzen
moan	Stöhnen
to writhe in unison	sich gemeinsam winden

Darkness had fallen and the fire's flickering blaze was their only light. Warm orange painted their skin as the flames in the fireplace danced like lovers.

By the time Alison finally pulled away from Luka's embrace, the fire's light was beginning to **dwindle**. Her mouth felt **raw** from his rough kisses, but there was still an aching hunger within her that was not yet satisfied.

to dwindle	dahinschwinden
raw	*hier:* wund
unspent	*hier:* anhaltend
to glisten	glänzen

Control yourself, for God's sake! she thought.

The room was getting dark and the air felt thick with **unspent** desire. Sensing that Alison was trying to calm things down, Luka slowly rose from the sofa, pulled his shirt back over his broad chest and began to add more wood to the fire.

Übung 18: Match-up. Verbinden Sie die Verben mit den passenden Substantiven!

1. ☐ paint   **a)** dagger

2. ☐ stab   **b)** heartbeat

3. ☐ quicken   **c)** canvases

4. ☐ make   **d)** light

5. ☐ dwindle   **e)** excuses

Alison breathed in slowly and deeply. Sweat **glistened** on her chest as it rose and fell in the near darkness. Calm down, she thought. What are you doing? You don't even know this man.

When the flames grew, Alison noticed in the firelight that her shirt was half open. She did it up quickly before Luka could turn around.

She felt suddenly shy and unsure.

"I... I'm not normally like that, by the way," she said, forcing a laugh. Luka turned around and walked over to the sofa to sit beside her. Very gently, he **cupped** the side of her face with his hand and looked at her with his piercing eyes.

"I liked it," he said softly. "A lot."

Alison's lips curved in a shy smile. "Me, too," she agreed, her voice almost a whisper.

Then, as though noticing the darkness for the first time, she added, "It's getting late."

Luka's expression seemed to lose some of its brightness. "Do you need to go home?"

"No, no, that's not what I was going to say," Alison replied quickly. "I mean, not unless you want me to?"

The dark pools of his eyes lit up when he heard that she was not leaving, and he did not need to answer her.

to cup	umfassen, die Hände legen um
to fumble for sth.	nach etw. tasten
flatly	ausdruckslos

"I just need to let my grandma know that I might not be back for a while, that's all," she continued. "Give me a minute; I'll send her a text message."

Alison **fumbled for** her phone in the bag that she had hastily dropped at the end of the sofa. She quickly typed out a message.

Eve would probably think nothing of her granddaughter staying late at Jenny's house, since she had done so many times in the past. It was barely necessary to invent a lie, but Alison explained that they were going to watch a few girly films and then have dinner.

Now that her thoughts had finally returned to more practical matters, that reminded her: "Maybe we should think about getting something to eat."

"Uh, yeah, we could do that," Luka replied **flatly**. "The Old Banner is just next door if you want to go out for dinner."

Alison thought about the lie that she had told her grandmother. In such a small village, she would surely be recognized in The Old Banner. Then, one way or another, Eve would find out where she had really been.

apprehensive	besorgt
chef	Köchin
artificial	künstlich
cutlery	Besteck

"I was thinking of something a little more intimate," she suggested quickly. "You know, just the two of us. I could cook something if you like?"

Luka looked apprehensive for a short moment.

"Don't worry, I'm a good cook!" Alison laughed, playfully slapping him on the arm.

"I'm sure you are," he said warmly. "I'm just not sure I have much food in the house. As I said, I don't have a lot of guests, and, well, I don't usually have the services of such a good chef as yourself…"

"Don't you cook for yourself?"

"I'm terrible at it," he explained. "I think all of my creativity must have been used up on drawing and painting."

"Never mind. You must have *something* that we can eat."

Übung 19: Common nouns. Lesen Sie weiter und unterstreichen Sie alle sieben Substantive im Text!

Alison stood up and moved to walk to the kitchen, ignoring the slight pull of Luka's hand around her wrist as she went. She switched on the lights and an artificial glow immediately replaced the golden firelight.

The kitchen had all the cutlery, pots and pans that could be expected. And yet, somehow, none of them seemed to be where anybody who regularly did any cooking would put them. Even the knives and forks were mixed with tin-openers and wooden spoons in a dusty pot on the table top.

"Men!" Alison laughed to herself as she opened the fridge.

"Wow, you really weren't joking, were you?" she remarked, seeing that it was almost empty. "Oh, hang on, I've found an onion."

She held out the withered vegetable like a rare and prized discovery.

Luka was still in the other room, but he unthinkingly reached out a hand as though to halt her raid of his barren kitchen. The gesture was small, but strangely desperate. She did not notice it and continued exploring the drawers and cupboards.

"I'm half expecting to find cobwebs in here!" she teased, pulling open the door of a wooden cupboard.

The rusty hinge squeaked loudly.

"Oh, well, you have tins at least. And... looks like... yes, it's spaghetti. That's a start. Ooh, garlic!"

withered	vertrocknet
⚡ prized	wertvoll, toll
raid	Plünderung
cobweb	Spinnweben
to tease	necken
hinge	Scharnier
to graze	streifen, leicht (an)kratzen

Alison was cheerfully beginning to assemble a rather pitiful pile of ingredients on the table top. She turned back towards Luka and put her hands on her hips.

"It won't be anything too special, but I could do spaghetti with a nice tomato sauce. How about it?"

Luka came to stand behind her, then weaved his arms through hers and squeezed her gently. He bent down so that his face rested against her cheek. Playfully, he took her earlobe in his mouth, grazing her flesh with his teeth.

"If you say so, my little chef," he teased. "Although I can think of things I'd rather do than eat."

Alison turned around and kissed him, then pulled his hands away and shot him a **mischievous** look.

"Well, yes, I think I can see from your bare cupboards that eating is not your top priority."

Their eyes **locked** for a moment, then Alison shifted her **gaze** back to the ingredients. She looked around the kitchen and eventually **retrieved** a forgotten chopping board from behind a stack of pans.

"Don't you have any sharp knives?" she asked as she searched through a dusty drawer.

"I'll find you one," he replied.

Before she knew it, the knife was in her hand, though she had not seen its hiding place. She unwrapped a piece of garlic from its dry skin and began to cut it into small **slivers**. The knife shimmered in the artificial light. Luka's face was reflected in its metallic shine; he seemed to be watching her carefully.

"Ouch!" Alison cried out.

Foolishly, she had been looking at the reflection in the knife instead of her fingers next to the sharp **blade**. Now she saw the deep cut on her finger. Blood was pouring over the chopping board, **splattering** the garlic with drops of red. It looks almost like a tomato sauce, she thought in shocked stupidity before remembering to apply pressure to the bleeding finger with her other hand. She felt suddenly **light-headed** and reached behind her for Luka's support.

"I've cut myself," she said weakly and turned around.

The face that she saw was not Luka's face. She heard her own scream fracture the silence and hang in the air as everything went into slow

mischievous	verschmitzt
to lock	*hier:* sich ineinander bohren
gaze	Blick
to retrieve	finden, aufspüren
sliver	Scheibchen
blade	Klinge
to splatter	(be)spritzen
light-headed	benommen, schwindelig

motion; her own movements seemed **agonizingly sluggish**. The knife was still lying on the chopping board, splattered with **ruby**-coloured drops of liquid. It took all her effort to pick it up.

agonizingly	qualvoll
sluggish	schleppend, träge
ruby	Rubin

Übung 20: Multiple choice. Kreuzen Sie die richtige Variante an!

1. The unusual thing about Luka's kitchen was that...
   a) ☐ he had no cutlery or cooking equipment.
   b) ☐ nothing was in quite the right place.
   c) ☐ everything was clean and in its place.

2. Alison offered to cook...
   a) ☐ spaghetti with tomato sauce.
   b) ☐ pasta with onions and garlic.
   c) ☐ cheese on toast.

3. Alison cut herself because...
   a) ☐ Luka was distracting her by talking to her.
   b) ☐ she was thinking too much about her feelings for Luka.
   c) ☐ she was looking at the reflection in the knife.

3 Bloodlust

No, no, no! This can't be happening, thought Luka.

All he had wanted to do was protect Alison. Now he saw her before him, her hands shaking as they gripped the bloody knife, and her screams echoing like an ache through his heart. How could he have let things get so out of control?

He felt the pointed **spikes** of his teeth graze his lips. They were glistening, pearl-white weapons that he had grown to **despise** a long time ago. More than ever, they felt like an **intrusion** in his mouth. **Despair** filled him blackly as he realized that his eyes would have turned to an **unearthly** silver, too. He should never have allowed Alison to get so close to him; he

bloodlust	Blutrausch
spike	Spitze
to despise	hassen, verachten
intrusion	*hier:* Fremdkörper
despair	Verzweiflung
unearthly	überirdisch, unheimlich

had known all along that the risk was too great. But her warmth against him and the sweet, wet taste of her mouth had made him feel almost human again.

"You monster!" Alison now screamed wildly.

She was right, Luka thought. She would never have let him touch her if she had known the darkness of his true nature. This was how she saw him: a monster. A blood-sucking Dracula. And how could he ever have expected any different?

Alison stood glued to the floor, holding the knife straight out in front of her as though ready to lunge forward and attack. She had seen everything. Luka turned away from her and tried to regain control. If only he could stop thinking about the smell of her blood…

"I don't want to hurt you, I promise."

The words sounded useless, but he could think of nothing better. Alison was still screaming, gripping the knife tightly. She sounded weak and frightened, and out of the corner of his eye Luka saw that her face was **crumpled** with terror. He **was** not **accustomed to** feeling pity, but he felt its bite now. Alison looked so scared that all he wanted to do was comfort her, but he knew that he could only make things worse. It was him that she was afraid of.

"I know what this must look like…"

Oh God, how **clichéd**.

"Alison, I am not going to hurt you," he said slowly.

"Liar!" she yelled **viciously**, her voice shrill and hysterical. "Stay away from me!"

"I never wanted to attack you, Alison. It's just the blood… it has this effect on me. But I'm not going to do anything – I don't hurt people."

crumpled	verzerrt
to be accustomed to	an etw. gewöhnt sein
clichéd	klischeehaft
viciously	*hier:* heftig
to curse oneself	sich verfluchen
thrill	Kick, Erregung
to stir	hervorrufen, erregen
to tear away	losreißen

It was more or less true, he thought: he did what he could to avoid causing pain.

Luka sighed deeply. "I'm going to stay exactly where I am. You can move as slowly as you want, and you can leave. The door's unlocked." Trembling like a frightened animal, Alison took a few steps towards the door, keeping her eyes fixed on Luka and holding the knife between the two of them the whole time. Blood was dripping from her hand onto the carpet in small, red splashes.

Luka **cursed himself** for the **thrill** of excitement the droplets **stirred** in him. He **tore away** his eyes and forced himself to focus on her terror. The terror that he had created.

The cut was bleeding heavily now and quiet tears were streaming down her face.

"Alison, you can leave if you want. Or you can stay."

Alison could feel her heartbeat vibrating through her entire body. It was pounding its rapid rhythm in her chest, her stomach, her arms and legs, reaching a crescendo of restless noise in her head. She had never been more aware of the beat that pushed blood around her own body.

She could leave, or she could stay. It was a simple choice, and yet in the fever of fear and adrenaline, there was no simple answer. Everything that she had ever

to pound	schlagen, hämmern
to doubt one's sanity	an seinem Verstand zweifeln
to compel	zwingen, drängen

known about the world seemed to have been turned upside down. Standing just metres away from her was a vampire.

A *vampire*!

It was impossible to believe, but she could see it with her own eyes. And her attacker yesterday – the madman – he must have been a vampire, too, she realized. Everything Luka had told her about that night must have been a lie.

Her thoughts were a blur, but within the confusion there was one thing that was definite: if Luka was dangerous, it would make very little difference whether she left or not. He knew that she was staying with her grandmother and could easily find her. And – even though it caused her to **doubt her sanity** – something was still **compelling** her to stay.

Übung 22: Contracted forms. Schreiben Sie die Sätze neu und verwenden Sie, wo möglich, die Kurzform der Verben!

1. It would not make much difference whether she stayed or left.

   _____

2. It is not just that I will not do it – I cannot do it.

   _____

3. But I am not going to do anything – I do not hurt people.

   _____

4. Luka was not accustomed to feeling pity, but he felt its bite now.

   _____

   _____

"I can heal your cut, if you'll trust me," Luka said after a few moments.

Alison laughed through the tears. "Trust you?!"

"Believe me. I'll show you that I don't mean you any harm. You can hold the knife right to my heart and stake me with it if I get too close. Just give me your finger."

He looked almost surprised at his own words, as though they had not been planned. His expression seemed to suggest that seeing her in pain was causing him discomfort.

harm	Schaden
to stake	aufspießen, pfählen
to flinch	(zusammen)zucken
sensation	Gefühl, Empfindung
palm	Handfläche
to dig	bohren, stoßen

"Alison, trust me. I wasn't lying about saving you yesterday. I'm not a killer. And I'm not lying when I tell you that I wish, more than you can ever know, that I wasn't like this, so that we could have just had a nice dinner together like two normal people."

Very slowly and carefully, Alison approached him with the knife extended in front of her. Luka did not flinch when she brought its sharp metal point to rest directly above his heart. Her eyes were wide with fear, but she was ready to stab the knife into his chest without warning.

"Give me your finger," he said softly.

"Is this some kind of trick?" she said. Her voice was quiet but firm.

"No."

Cautiously, she placed her hand in his.

Das Substantiv **point** bedeutet nicht nur Punkt, sondern bezeichnet auch die (scharfe) Spitze von Objekten, hier eine Messerspitze.

He felt the warm, wet sensation of blood dripping into his palm. This was too important for him to allow himself to lose control.

Luka slowly moved her hand towards his mouth and felt Alison flinch. She dug the blade a little harder into his chest.

"I promise," he said, looking into Alison's eyes.

Übung 23: Past tense forms. Lesen Sie weiter und unterstreichen Sie alle zwölf Vergangenheitsformen!

He quickly licked up the blood with his tongue. It was not what she had been expecting him to do, and she pulled her hand away instinctively. But somehow, when she looked at her hand, she saw the cut healing completely in front of her eyes. After half a minute, the only sign that it had ever been there at all was the spilled blood that remained on the carpet. She took a few steps back and the relief showed on her face. "You can still leave," Luka said softly.

But Alison let herself follow her instinct. Whatever strange and incredible world she now found herself in, she could not turn away. Not now.

She sat down on the sofa, and almost immediately the questions started to fall from her lips.

"What *are* you, Luka?!" she began.

"You know what I am, Alison."

He took a seat at the other end of the sofa and looked at her with his large, black eyes. His fangs were disappearing back into his mouth and a quiet calmness was slowly returning to his face.

"Then, how... how did you open the door to me this afternoon when it was still light? Doesn't sunlight burn you? And the garlic..."

"You shouldn't believe everything you see in horror films," Luka laughed blackly. "Garlic has no effect on me, other than making my breath smell. And I could quite happily look at crosses and bathe in holy water if I wanted to. You're right, though, sunlight does burn my skin. But I can stand it for a few minutes without serious injury."

"And the man who attacked me yesterday, was he a vampire, too?" Alison asked.

"Yes, he was. I'm sorry I had to lie to you about that. He was just a stupid junkie – a newly made vampire. It takes some time for vampires to take control of their thirst when they are first turned. Bloodlust overwhelms them, you see. They take too many risks."

Luka's eyes narrowed in anger and he looked away for a moment. But Alison did not rest in her questioning. "Is he still out there, preying on humans?"

Luka answered sharply. "Don't worry – I've dealt with that problem."

"But Luka, you can't let him..."

"I said, I've *dealt* with him."

Luka's expression made it clear that he would not discuss the issue further.

"Alison, look," he continued in a softer tone. "I'm sorry you got

to be turned (into a vampire)	zum Vampir gemacht werden
to overwhelm	überwältigen
to wipe	*hier:* (aus)löschen
matter-of-factly	sachlich, nüchtern
resistant	widerstandsfähig, immun
revulsion	Ekel
pawn	Marionette, Spielball

caught up in this. And the blackout... that honestly wasn't my intention. Something went wrong."

"What? What do you mean?"

"I couldn't let you tell anyone what had happened to you," Luka replied. "Our very existence is a secret that we must protect at all costs."

"Do you mean it was *you* who made me lose my memory?"

"Yes," Luka said simply and paused.

"And what did you mean when you said that 'something went wrong'?"

"Well, normally I can wipe a person's memory completely using simple mind tricks," Luka explained matter-of-factly. "It's a skill that all vampires have and that helps us to live among people unnoticed. But your mind was resistant. I must have gone too far trying to force you to forget, because the next thing I knew you had passed out.

That was never meant to happen. Besides, you know for yourself that your memories were not properly erased."

Alison looked at the calm face of the vampire with **revulsion**. He talked about her life and her memories as though she was little more than a **pawn** in his game. And how could she even know that he was not still lying to her now?

Übung 24: Word spiral. Fügen Sie die unten beschriebenen Wörter in die Wortspirale ein!

1	2	3	4	5	6	7
22	23	24	25	26	27	8
21	36	37	38	39	28	9
20	35	42	41	40	29	10
19	34	33	32	31	30	11
18	17	16	15	14	13	12

1-9: A feeling of extreme disgust.

9-14: The opposite of wide.

14-17: Luka tried to ... Alison's memories.

17-23: Something formerly hidden that is (suddenly) revealed or shown is ...

23-29: A feeling of complete hopelessness.

29-31: To tear apart or split open.

31-34: The inside of the hand, between the wrist and the fingers.

34-39: A mad person with wild behaviour.

39-42: A professional cook.

"My mind isn't a toy for you to play with!" she **snarled** with disgust. "You're saying these things as if they're just cold hard facts, but this is my *life* you're talking about. Or can't you understand that? Are you so dead inside that you don't even remember what it's like to have real thoughts and feelings?"

"I do have feelings," Luka replied, but his voice still sounded cold. "Although it sometimes seems like I feel them through a mile of water. They're just distant echoes most of the time. But, that... that wasn't how I felt earlier."

The memory of touching him made Alison feel sick.

"I would never have let you near me if you hadn't tricked me," she **spat**. "I can't believe that I actually thought I liked you!"

to snarl	wütend knurren
to spit	*hier:* fauchen
to bore into sb. (eyes)	jmd. mit den Augen durchbohren
to drag	ziehen, schleifen
conflicting	widersprüchlich
to run riot	verrücktspielen
in secrecy	im Verborgenen
to stiffen	sich versteifen
to feed	sich ernähren

The words had slipped out. Half of her wanted to pull them straight back out of the air; the other half wanted to see how Luka would respond.

"It wasn't a trick," he replied. "I like you, too."

His melancholy black eyes **bore into** her until she felt that she had to look away.

"Look," Luka continued, "I don't expect you to feel any sympathy for me. But you asked earlier whether I ever get lonely here without any visitors, and the answer is yes, Alison, I do. Of course I wish that I could just once, for *one single day*, truly feel close to somebody like you. When I wiped your memory, I was trying to protect you. That's why I told you that we hadn't met when you turned up at my door today... I wanted to keep you away from all of this. There's a world of daylight out there for you. I never wanted to **drag** you into the dark."

Alison sighed quietly. A hundred **conflicting** emotions were **running riot** inside her and she had no idea what to think. On the one hand, he had lied to her, played with her mind and hidden his true self from view. On the other, even in her anger, she could see that he had not attacked her, not even when she was an easy victim in his own home; he had even tried to protect her in his own strange way. He seemed to be speaking from his heart now, or whatever was left of it. And the things he was telling her, his very nature, in fact, were so fascinating that there was no way that she could drag herself away.

Übung 25: Choose the correct word. Lesen Sie weiter und unterstreichen Sie den passenden Begriff!

"Okay," she **1.** began / concluded . "And now that I know

2. something / everything , are you planning to **3.** erase /

lose all my memories of you?"

"I don't suppose that you'd **4.** let / get me," Luka replied,

with a raised **5.** smile / eyebrow .

"But you **6.** would / should do it anyway?"

"Of course I would, Alison. Tomorrow you'll be gone, but I'll still be a vampire. And I'll still be in danger if you tell anyone about me. I've lived in secrecy for so long; there's no other way for me to survive." Alison stiffened. She stood up straight and looked him in the eye. "I need to know something else," she said. "How do you feed? Where do you get your blood?"

"I feed from humans." His words were very firm, spoken with a hardness that masked a hint of regret. "But I do not kill them."

"But you have killed, in the past?"

"A long time ago," Luka replied flatly.

His eyes flickered with pain, and he paused.

"Like I told you, new vampires are like junkies: their thirst for blood is ravenous and unending. In the first few weeks after I was born to the darkness, I was much like the vampire who attacked you yesterday – barely more than an animal. But I haven't killed since then."

"Then how do you get humans to give you their blood?"

Luka laughed gently.

"Trust me, it's not too hard to find a donor. It can be quite a... pleasurable experience to be bitten."

"What?!" Alison exclaimed, disbelief written across her face.

"It's like a seduction. Like the most sensual kiss. The pain is only momentary, and then there's an intense

ravenous	unbändig, unstillbar
donor	(Blut-)Spender
seduction	Verführung
rush	Ansturm, Rausch
to snap	*hier:* blaffen
remnant	Rest, Überbleibsel
unflinching	unbeirrbar, entschlossen

rush of sensation and it feels like you could lose yourself in it completely. Of course, I make my donors forget all about it afterwards."

A terrible thought suddenly flashed into Alison's head like lightning. "Wait a minute, you weren't going to bite me earlier, were you? You didn't think of me as a... donor?!"

Luka shook his head firmly.

"No. I was never going to take a bite. I wouldn't have trusted myself."

"So what happened between us wasn't part of your usual seduction?"

A corner of Luka's mouth curved upwards into a half-smile. "I can enjoy other human pleasures, if that's what you're wondering."

"I was certainly not wondering that!" Alison snapped.

Now that she knew that the ruggedly handsome man in front of her was not even human, there could surely be no remnant of the hot desire that she had felt earlier. Could there?

She decided to change the subject quickly.

"So... Tell me... How were you made into a vampire?"

Luka turned away, seemingly lost in thought.

"There's only one way to be made like me. A vampire fed on me until my human self died, and then she offered me her own blood. I drank from her, and I awoke to a new life of darkness."

"That's terrible!" came Alison's small, shrill voice. "Why did she do it to you?"

Luka looked at her, **unflinching**. "Because I asked her to."

Übung 26: Questions to the text. Beantworten Sie die Fragen zum Text in ganzen Sätzen!

1. What explanation does Luka give for having killed in the past?

   _____

   _____

2. What word does Luka use to describe a human whom he feeds from?

   _____

3. Why is it not hard for Luka to find someone to feed from?

   _____

   _____

4. What has to happen for a human to become a vampire?

   _____

   _____

Luka felt a shadow pass over him. The events he was describing had taken place over three hundred years ago, but he still felt them more sharply than any of the countless nights that had passed since then.

smooth	glatt, weich
scarlet	scharlachrot
uncompre-hendingly	verständnislos
to trigger sth.	etw. wecken, auslösen
bleak	trostlos, kalt
to affect	(negativ) be-einflussen

He did not need to close his eyes to see the vampire's face in front of him. Her skin was so pale and smooth, and a thin scarlet line like a string of rubies ran down one side of her mouth...

Alison looked at him uncomprehendingly.

"But why? Why would you ask her to turn you into a monster?"

"You have to understand that my life was very hard back then. Unfortunately, I couldn't have known how much harder it would get."

Alison's question had triggered a vivid memory in Luka's mind. He remembered, as if it was only yesterday, carrying a bucket in his rough hands as he walked towards the river. His body ached[i] from the day's hard work at the small farm his father had built on the muddy piece of land beside their home. That was all that life offered in this desolate nowhere: hard work. Hard work and death. Luka had so far escaped the second option, but he had lost three brothers, and his wife and newborn child had died only a month before.

To ache oder **to hurt**?

Im Englischen beschreibt **to ache** einen eher dumpfen, anhaltenden Schmerz, während **to hurt** sich eher auf einen stechenden Schmerz bezieht, oft aufgrund einer Verletzung.

As he walked nearer, he could see the river weaving between the shadowy trees in the moonlight. And then he saw an unearthly figure standing beside it. Her skin was so white that it was almost shining, and she was completely, unnaturally still.

Luka was immediately reminded of his parents' warning to him as a young boy: never enter the woods after dark, for wild creatures of the night hunt there. But his heart was too empty to feel fear.

The woman's cold hand gripped his as she led him into the forest. He had agreed to this. It was too late to change his mind now. For days, filled with bleak despair, he had let her take his blood. It had made him feel alive, ecstatic even, for just a few moments.

And then she had told him what he could become; how he could escape this misery and never again feel the full depth of human pain.

Übung 27: Unscramble. Lesen Sie weiter und ordnen Sie den Buchstabensalat zu sinnvollen Wörtern!

"Who was the other **1.** verpiam _____?"

Alison asked, disturbing the **2.** nesec _____

that had formed, unwanted, in Luka's mind.

"A traveller, who had come across from **3.** Handoll

_____ in search of new **4.** dobol _____.

Joanna van den Driessche was her name; I still remember

her face as **5.** rylacel _____ as I can see yours

now. So **6.** ulfiatube _____, pale and cruel."

"Did you ever see her again?" Alison asked.

"I did, yes. She affected my life in a lot of ways, as it happens. But she died centuries ago."

Alison shuddered. "How... how old are you?"

"As a man, I lived until I was twenty-eight."

"And as a... as a vampire, how long have you lived?"

"I don't celebrate birthdays," he replied icily. "I became a vampire in 1693, so... you can work it out."

Luka turned away again.

His mind was back in the forest on the last night of his human life... The deal had been made, and there was no turning back.

Joanna laughed childishly, then suddenly she jumped and let out a violent hiss. Her fangs were extended and her eyes flashed with a terrible silver light. She bit Luka, but there was no pleasure this time, only pain. Within moments he was **pinned to the ground** and struggling to get free, but his efforts quickly became sluggish as the blood drained from his body.

"Poor baby," she **taunted**.

Her white face was **illuminated** in the moonlight and he saw his own scarlet blood spill down her chin. Suddenly the attack was over, and

to pin sb. to the ground	jmd. am Boden festhalten
to taunt	spotten, höhnen
to illuminate	erleuchten, er-hellen
to come unstuck	*hier:* aus den Fugen geraten
to unfold	enthüllt werden
companion-ship	Gesellschaft

she punctured her own wrist. A few drops of blood fell towards his lips.

Consciousness was slipping away. With his last breath, he did the only thing that would not mean death: he drank from her, almost gratefully.

In that instant, darkness ripped through him. He felt his senses sharpen and his teeth grow so pointed that he cut his tongue upon them. And then he felt an overwhelming new sensation blocking out everything else: an enormous, ravenous thirst.

Übung 28: Reported speech. Wie lauten die folgenden Sätze in der direkten Rede?

1. Alison asked who the other vampire was.

   _____

2. Luka said that he could still see her face now.

   _____

3. Alison asked if Luka ever saw her again.

   _____

4. The vampire had died a long time ago, Luka explained.

   _____

Alison listened with shock and disbelief to his words. 1693 – that made Luka over three hundred years old. It was impossible!

She doubted so much of what she had seen and heard over the past day that it felt as if reality had come unstuck. Even now, when the most unlikely of all explanations seemed to be unfolding before her eyes, there were still so many things that did not make sense. She could not stop herself from asking more questions.

"Have *you* ever turned someone into a vampire?"

Luka's face grew as hard as stone. "Once, but it was a terrible mistake."

"Why did you do it?"

"Because he wanted it so much, and foolishly, selfishly, I thought that it would mean some kind of companionship for me. Over the centuries I have taken up just about every hobby there is – I've taught myself to play dozens of instruments, and I can speak twenty languages fluently... but there is no substitute for companionship."

"What went wrong?"

"He didn't turn out like me. He never learnt to control his blood-lust, though I tried so hard to teach him. I wish that I had killed him when I had the chance."

Alison looked up at the stony face of the vampire. She could never begin to imagine the life that he had led or the emotions that flickered dimly in the darkness of his soul. Yet she sensed that he was opening up to her more fully and honestly than he had done in many years. And beneath the power and the danger, she could see through to the loneliness of his existence.

She was no longer afraid.

Übung 29: Translation. Ergänzen Sie die Sätze mit der passenden Übersetzung!

| erhellt | fauchte | Ersatz | verspotteten |

1. There is no ⬚⬚⬚⬚⬚⬚⬚ for companionship.

2. The vampire's face was ⬚⬚⬚⬚⬚⬚ in the moonlight.

3. Her mocking words ⬚⬚⬚⬚⬚⬚ him.

4. Joanna ⬚⬚⬚⬚⬚⬚ as she attacked Luka.

What madness was this? He must have lost his mind, Luka thought, to be telling all the secrets that he had guarded for centuries to a girl he barely knew.

He of all people should know the importance of secrecy. His first years as a vampire had coincided with a mass hysteria against his kind that spread across the countryside of Europe like a raging fire. His own village in the Serbian mountains did not escape its fever: stakings and grave diggings soon became common.

Yes, it was true that he had good reasons for secrecy. He could still smell the flames that had ripped through the old watermill where he had made his first home as a vampire. That scorching scent of danger that drove him out of his homelands and into a life spent on the run…

substitute	Ersatz
to coincide	zusammenfallen, sich überschneiden mit
raging	lodernd, tobend
scorching	*hier:* beißend
to open the floodgates	die Schleusen öffnen

And yet there was something about Alison that seemed to make him lose control of his senses. He had opened the floodgates now, and his whole life was pouring out for her to see. He could not bear to think how it must disgust her.

"If I could go back and change what I am, I would do it in an instant," he said suddenly.

The way that he looked at her gave her no reason to doubt him.

"I can see that," she responded softly. "Luka, I understand why you had to lie to me… But now that I think about it, I can't understand why you're telling me the truth now."

"I don't understand that either," he answered. "Something just… takes hold of me when I'm around you."

As though to prove his point, Luka suddenly bent down and kissed her passionately on the lips. She pulled back for a moment but then returned the kiss, tentatively at first, and then with the full force of her desire.

Eventually, Alison stood back. She put her hand over her mouth and looked up with confusion and shock in her eyes.

"This… this can't happen," she said. "I should go."

Luka's rough hands were around her waist, but she broke free of him, grabbed her bag and hurried towards the door. When she reached it, she turned and looked at him with what looked, just for a moment, like regret.

She left without saying a word.

gust	Stoß, Böe
slender	schlank
roar	Gebrüll

Luka opened his mouth to speak, but before the words could escape a **gust** of wind blew the door shut behind Alison. It closed with a loud bang. All he could do was watch her **slender** figure grow smaller through the window, then disappear into the night. He sighed deeply.

He had lived in this barren, weather-beaten village for five years. He looked around the home that he had made for himself: the stacks of drawings and paintings meant nothing to him; the books that had been his only company on so many long nights offered little comfort now.

Packing would not take long, he concluded. He could leave before Alison had a chance to tell everyone his dark secret – before the flames and the angry **roar** of villagers came to follow him once again.

Übung 30: True or false? Kreuzen Sie die richtigen Aussagen an!

1. Luka's first home as a vampire was destroyed by angry villagers. ☐

2. Luka opened up to Alison because he was tired of living in secrecy. ☐

3. Alison still cannot trust anything that Luka says to her. ☐

4. Luka won't miss any of his possessions. ☐

 4 Dark City

Alison walked towards the high street ahead, which was shrouded in a thick fog. The fog was lit up dimly by the streetlights behind, and above it all the thin moon was surrounded by a shining halo of cloud. She had finally reached her own neighbourhood in London after a long journey back from the Highlands, where the last few hours of her holiday had passed in a blur.

Walking past the familiar shops and takeaway restaurants and finally onto her own street, she felt relieved to be almost home.

On her way back, Alison had been thinking about the events of the past

to shroud	einhüllen
halo	Heiligenschein
to inhabit	*hier:* durchleben
to acknow-ledge	anerkennen, zugeben

two days constantly. She had thought long and hard about everything that had happened, and yet she had not shared any of her thoughts or memories with anyone. It was strange, she thought, but somehow Luka's secret had now become her own.

She felt sure that the reason she had not told anyone about her dark discovery had something to do with the way that Luka had put his trust in her: she did not know why he had shared so much of the knowledge that could destroy him. Intuition told her that, in the three centuries that he had inhabited, Luka must rarely have allowed himself to be so vulnerable.

But that was not the only reason that she had kept his secret to herself. Hiding in the back of her consciousness was a feeling that she could barely bring herself to acknowledge: she had really felt something for him. She felt it still. And his incredible story had left her longing for more. Even though she knew what he was now, her attraction to him had not gone away. If anything, it was stronger than ever. Nobody would believe her if she told them about him anyway, she thought. Even her closest friends would surely think that she was mad, or assume that it was some sort of sick joke.

mist	Nebel
to head straight towards	direkt zusteuern auf
insistently	nachdrücklich
sickening	entsetzlich

Alison breathed in the cold freshness of the night air and breathed out a cloud of mist. Her home was not far away, and she felt suddenly desperate to return to the simple routine of her normal life. At least that way the events that had turned her life upside down might eventually become nothing more than a distant memory. London could not be more unlike the Scottish village she had left earlier that day, and now, back in her own territory, everything that had happened to her in the Highlands felt like a very strange dream.

But it had happened. There was no way that she could fool herself into forgetting that creatures from her worst nightmares walked the streets of the real world.

She continued walking quickly through the fog. She could barely see the first few houses in front of her, let alone [i] her own, which was at the very end of the long street. Suddenly, through the cloudy fog that surrounded her, a dark figure appeared, little more than a silhouette. As the person came into the light, she could see that it was a man dressed in black.

Die Wendung **let alone** (geschweige denn, ganz zu schweigen von) verstärkt wie die deutsche Entsprechung eine negative Aussage.

He was walking very quickly, and – she looked again to make sure – yes, he seemed to be heading straight towards her. Panicking, she froze. Her heartbeat pounded insistently. Run, it said. Run now!

Übung 31: Pronouns. Schreiben Sie die Sätze neu und ersetzen Sie die markierten Satzteile mit dem passenden Pronomen!

1. **Alison** breathed in the cold freshness **of the night air.**

   _____

2. **London** could not be any less like the Highland village **Alison** had left earlier that day.

   _____

   _____

3. **Her friends** would not believe **Alison** anyway.

   _____

4. **The unknown man** was walking towards **Alison**.

   _____

The stranger was coming closer and Alison was filled with a **sickening** sense of déjà vu as she waited for the attack. He was only a few footsteps away, still coming towards her, closer, closer, and then he was... gone. He had walked straight past her, opened the gate that led to a tidy garden in the row of houses beside her and turned his key in the door.

While Alison was standing frozen like a frightened statue on the pavement, her 'attacker' lifted up his young daughter to greet her and then moved to close the door behind him.

Alison felt extremely foolish. Her heart was still beating wildly and her breath was short and loud. Pull yourself together! she thought to herself, finally breaking free of the paralysis. And yet she realized now that what had happened in Scotland would not be as easy to forget as she had hoped. Luka was not the only vampire out there. Overnight, the world that she knew had become much more dangerous and uncertain.

She tried to ignore her fear, but she could not help but walk unnaturally quickly towards home. She was almost running by the time her small, shabby house appeared through the heavy mist ahead. It had always looked a little out of place among the neat family homes all around it, but as Alison approached, she thought it had never looked more welcoming.

Finally, she was at the front door and was fumbling in her purse for the key. Before she could put it in the keyhole, though, the door opened right in front of her.

"You're home at last!" exclaimed a pretty, brown-haired girl.

She was holding out a tray of freshly baked biscuits; the delicious smell was wafting out into the street to greet Alison.

Alison felt so pleased to see her

paralysis	Lähmung
neat	nett, akkurat
to waft	wehen
housemate	Mitbewohnerin
exterior	Äußeres
to radiate	ausstrahlen

housemate Jess that she ran forward and hugged her, almost knocking the tray out of her hand.

"Are these for me?" she asked gratefully.

"Oh, you know me. When I'm bored, I bake," Jess remarked casually. "...And I clean!"

She gestured proudly at the room behind her, which Alison had to agree looked wonderful. Colourful cushions were neatly arranged on the sofas, and books and films were lined in tidy rows on the shelves. The soft, feminine colours inside the house were nothing like its shabby exterior; every detail seemed to radiate comfort and familiarity.

Home, sweet home, Alison thought to herself.

Übung 32: Opposites. Lesen Sie weiter und setzen Sie die Gegenteile der markierten Begriffe ein!

"It's so **1.** bad _____ to be back," Alison sighed

as she collapsed onto the **2.** painful _____ sofa.

Jess put the tray of biscuits on the coffee table and

sat **3.** up _____ beside her.

"I'm not surprised. I still can't believe you **4.** refused

_____ to spend your week off in the Scottish

Highlands! What about, oh, I don't know... somewhere less

5. boiling _____ and miserable than London?"

"You know that I haven't got the money to go anywhere nice, not with what they pay us at Apex," Alison reminded her. "And anyway, I like to keep my gran company from time to time. I think she must get lonely up there in the middle of nowhere, now that all the rest of the family has gone south."

"So, how was it?"

Alison tried to speak, but the words got stuck in her throat. Jess was her best friend, and she could not imagine lying to her. But it was impossible to find the right words to describe the holiday.

Moreover, it also felt as if something, perhaps an instinct, was stopping her.

"It was... fine."

"Wow! Sounds eventful! I wish I'd gone with you."

Alison laughed uneasily at her friend's sarcasm, then changed the subject.

"It's pretty foggy outside, have you seen?"

Jess **squinted** her eyes and looked at Alison **suspiciously**.

"Did something happen up in Scotland? You're acting strangely."

"Uh, no, everything's fine," Alison replied.

eventful	ereignisreich
to squint	die Augen zusammenkneifen
suspiciously	misstrauisch
⚡ crap liar	lausige Lügnerin
brightly	*hier:* fröhlich
⚡ to be on sb.'s back	jmd. im Nacken sitzen
sales policy	Verkaufsstrategie

"I can tell you're lying," Jess said with concern in her voice. "You know you're a crap liar."

Alison laughed.

"You're right, Sherlock. To tell the truth it was a little bit weird. I had this blackout... just collapsed outside my grandma's house. I couldn't remember a thing about what had happened, so it was pretty scary."

She hoped that this half-truth would satisfy Jess's curiosity.

"Oh no, that sounds awful! Did you find out what caused it?"

"No, actually," Alison tried to dismiss the subject with an uneasy laugh. "But the doctor said I was fine. They did tests and everything. It just frightened me a bit at the time. Anyway, what have you been up to while I've been gone? Apart from cleaning, I mean."

"And baking," Jess replied, more **brightly**. "Don't forget the baking. But... other than that... not that much. Work's been rubbish without you. Margaret's still complaining because they've cancelled the office party, and Tim's **been on my back** all week checking that I'm following the new **sales policy** on every call."

Übung 33: Unscramble the dialogue. Lesen Sie weiter und bringen Sie die Sätze in die richtige Reihenfolge!

a) "Thanks, Jess."

b) "...And I haven't even learned the new policy yet. Oh, it's going to be awful..."

c) Alison's mood instantly slumped. "Oh no, don't remind me... I really wish I didn't have to go back on Monday..."

d) Jess looked sympathetic. "I'll make you a nice cup of tea. A cup of tea makes everything better."

e) "Don't we all, don't we all."

1	2	3	4	5

Alison looked up gratefully into Jess's warm, friendly expression. She felt as if the moment to say anything about Luka had passed. The secret was burning inside her, and she longed to talk about the conflicting feelings that he had stirred in her. But to say anything to anyone might lead to him being discovered and harmed. And despite the confusion of her feelings about him, she could not bear for that to happen.

A tall, slender man turned to Luka and looked at him firmly.
"All right, all right, if you really have nowhere else to go, then I'll have to agree to it. But you cannot stay on my territory for long. You must know that, Luka."

The man moved with an effortless grace that made him look light and unearthly beneath the harsh fluorescent lighting of the hospital ward. "Thank you," Luka whispered.

"Look," the other man continued. "I just need to finish up here and then I can take you back to my place. Wait outside, and for God's sake, try to stay out of trouble for five minutes."

The man's eyes flashed with irritation, but he managed a small smile in Luka's direction as he turned back towards the sleeping patients. Luka watched him collect two bedpans and carry them out of a double door at the end of the ward.

Moments later, he was standing outside the hospital, looking in through a window that opened out onto a quiet, dark area of the car park. This would be his last view of his workplace, Inverness General Hospital.

It was a shame really, he thought. The job had suited him well: it was ordinary enough not to attract attention, and people didn't ask questions about his preference for night shifts. Besides, there was so much blood kept in storage that the odd pouch that went missing was never noticed. He and his friend Graham had always been careful not to steal from work supplies too often or too much, so nobody had ever noticed anything unusual.

Graham quickly returned to the half-open window where Luka was looking in from the darkness.

"Okay, I'm ready," Graham said. "I'll come and meet you outside."

It was 4 a.m. and the roads were empty as they drove towards the remote cottage, just north of Inverness.

"I hope you know the danger that you're putting me in by staying with me," Graham growled angrily.

ward	Station (Kranken-haus)
irritation	Verärgerung
bedpan	Bettpfanne
preference	Vorliebe
in storage	auf Vorrat, auf Lager
odd	*hier:* gelegentlich
pouch	*hier:* Blutkonserve
supplies *pl*	Vorräte, Material

"I do, and I can't thank you enough for agreeing to it."

"Like I said, it won't be for long."

"I just need a couple of days to work out what I'm going to do next."

Graham shook his head as though he was disappointed in his friend.

"How did it happen, Luka? How could you let it happen?"

aggravated	genervt, aufgebracht
to wager	wetten (veraltet)
the hows and whys	das Wie und Warum
to persist	beharren, insistieren
to concede	zugeben, einräumen

Luka shot him an aggravated look. "I already told you. Her mind was resistant – how should I know why wiping her memory didn't work? Then she came back to find me. I tried to keep her away, believe me."

"Not hard enough, I'll wager."

Luka felt a stab of irritation. He hated how Graham sometimes used such old-fashioned phrases. Luka always made an effort not to let his speech give away his age, so why couldn't he?

"Well, Graham, you bet wrong. Anyway, it's happened now, so I just need to work out what to do about it. Endlessly talking about the hows and whys of the situation is completely pointless."

Luka heard the hardness in his voice and breathed in deeply to calm himself down.

"Do you think that she'll go to the newspapers?" Graham persisted.

"I don't know, but I can't see any reason why not," Luka conceded sadly.

"Oh, this is bad. This is very bad. You'll have to keep out of sight for a few days while we find out just how big this story gets. Hopefully they won't believe the girl; they'll think she's just another village idiot with a crazy lie to sell to the papers. Like when old Thomas was outed in the Edinburgh Gazette and the journalist who wrote the article was practically laughed out of town."

Luka nodded his head. "Let's hope so."

But there was little hope in his heart.

Übung 34: Adjective or adverb? Vervollständigen Sie den Text mit dem fehlenden Adjektiv oder Adverb!

1. Hopeful _____ they won't believe the girl; they'll think that she's telling a crazy _____ lie to the papers.

2. Luka heard the hardness in his voice and breathed in deep _____ to calm himself down.

3. Well, Graham, you bet wrong _____.

4. The job had suited him good _____.

Monday morning at work was no better than Alison had feared. Her boss, Tim, had called her into his office twice before she had even had a chance to read the thirty pages of new guidelines. The booklet was still lying unopened on top of her in-tray. Apparently, she had been using the wrong type of language while on the phone to customers. By saying "no problem", she had implied that there possibly *could* have been a problem, and that was against the new policy. She looked over at Jess, whose desk was on the other side of the office, covered in photos. Alison mimed the action of shooting herself in the head, and Jess nodded in silent agreement. Above Jess's desk, the hands of the clock were moving into position: 10 a.m. Alison sighed. This could not be further from the world that Luka inhabited, she reflected with an involuntary shiver. Just thinking about Luka seemed to stir up a whirlpool of conflicting emotions in her: fear, excitement, revulsion, lust. His reality was no place for a human, and yet she still felt a strange longing to explore it further. Despite the danger, that world seemed so much more alive than this colourless place.

Her thoughts were interrupted by the shrill voice of Margaret, who had appeared suddenly at her desk.

"Did you hear?" squawked the voice. "They're cancelling the office party!"

Alison stopped staring into space and looked at her visitor. She realized that she had been doodling Luka's name on her notebook without thinking and instinctively reached to cover it with her hand.

"Uh, yeah, that's pretty bad. Everyone was looking forward to it, I guess."

This encouraged Margaret to continue with her topic, and Alison soon wished for an escape.

"Uh, Margaret… sorry, but I really have to learn the new policy before I get into any more trouble with Tim."

The older woman looked disappointed but returned to her desk, still mumbling to herself about the cancelled party.

in-tray	Posteingang(sfach)
to imply	andeuten
to mime	nachahmen
whirlpool	Wirbel, Strudel
to squawk	quäken
to doodle	vor sich hin kritzeln
half-heartedly	halbherzig

Half-heartedly, Alison picked up the policy booklet from where she had left it in her messy in-tray and let it fall open in front of her. *How to turn "no" into "yes"* was the title at the top of the page. She tried to read it, but soon found herself going over the same sentence for the fifth time without taking in a single word. She could not imagine anything more boring.

Alison sighed and let her head sink into her hands. Perhaps returning to her normal life was not such a good thing, after all. For a tiny, irrational moment, she wished she was back in Scotland, locked in the unearthly passion of a vampire's kiss.

Übung 35: Crossword puzzle. Lösen Sie das Kreuzwort-rätsel!

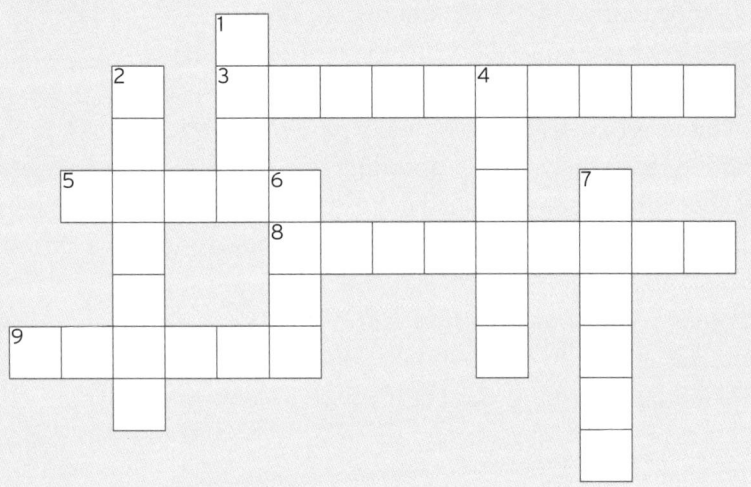

Down

1. To act out using gestures instead of words.
2. The best-known vampire ever.
4. A container for new work on an office desk.
6. A red gemstone.
7. To tremble with cold, fear or excitement.

Across

3. Not based on logic or reason.
5. An old-fashioned word meaning to bet.
8. Not of this world.
9. A set of guidelines or instructions for workers to follow.

Luka awoke just before dark, but allowed himself to open the curtains for a moment. The sun was setting, leaving a **burst** of red splashed across the sky like a **bloodstain**.

He felt the prickle of the faint sun on his skin, and the intense pain in his eyes that always came with looking into natural light. Squinting, he persisted. He rarely saw any sunlight, and tonight he felt unusually aware of its beauty.

He was still staring out of the window into the growing night when Graham opened the door.

"What are you doing?" Graham asked, a little aggravated.

"Calm down, it's dark already," Luka replied softly. "Don't you ever miss the sun?"

"Hmm, do I miss the sun, which burns and destroys me? Uh, no. Anyway, I thought I'd go and get the evening newspapers and find out whether you're Scotland's latest celebrity. I don't suppose I need to tell you to stay here."

"No, you don't," Luka growled.

Graham turned quickly and gracefully, and was gone in an instant. Alone again, Luka began to think.

burst	Lodern, Explosion
bloodstain	Blutfleck
prickle	Kribbeln
to justify	rechtfertigen
to wrinkle	(sich) runzeln

What would he do? Where would he go? And what on earth had compelled him to risk everything by telling his life story to a human girl he would never see again? He tried to justify himself: it was not his fault that she had remembered his name, or that she had come to his home. But he had not sent her away. And he had been an idiot to lose control and let her see his true nature.

His forehead wrinkled with irritation as he put his hands to his head, cursing himself for his stupidity. But even as he did so, the memory of Alison's touch and her warm, sweet scent came back to him and filled his heart with longing. The sensation made him feel even more foolish. He was a foolish, stupid – what was the word she had used? – monster. That was all he could ever be to her.

It was best not to let his mind wander when he was in a mood like this, he realized. Better to explore the house until Graham returned.

residence	Wohnhaus, Domizil
to relieve	*hier:* abhelfen, mildern
to board up	mit Brettern zunageln
revelation	Enthüllung

But the interior was no more comforting than that of Luka's own house; his friend made even less of an attempt than he did to make his home look like a human **residence**. The kitchen lay empty, unused, and its linoleum floor was brown at the edges, curling like old newspaper. There was no central heating to **relieve** the chill that neither of them felt, and the fireplace was **boarded up** with wood. Even the colour of the walls was dark.

Übung 36: Translation. Lesen Sie weiter und übersetzen Sie den Abschnitt ins Deutsche!

Luka felt relieved when Graham eventually returned, threw the papers at him and waited for a reaction.

Luka hurriedly searched through them one by one. Each time he picked up a newspaper, he expected to see Alison's **revelation** screaming out of the black and white headlines.

_____

_____

_____

_____

_____

_____

Luka examined the front pages carefully, but they told their usual stories of crime, sport or government mistakes, and the pictures were of nobody he recognized. He was looking in more detail now: still nothing.

"Have you already read through these?" Luka asked, still staring at the pages in front of him.

"Not every word, no, but I've taken a good look."

Graham pushed the paper from Luka's hand and looked at him, grinning from ear to ear.

"Seems like you've gotten away with it, you lucky **scoundrel**!"

This time Graham's old-fashioned vocabulary did not bother Luka at all. Had they not believed Alison, perhaps? Or had she guarded his secret **deliberately**? It was too much to hope for.

"It's only been a day. We can't celebrate yet," he said **soberly**.

"I certainly can't celebrate yet," Graham agreed. "I've got you hiding away here, whether or not the newspapers are onto it. When are you leaving?"

Luka knew not to expect a warm welcome from another vampire and was not surprised by Graham's cold words. He knew that Graham was particularly territorial and liked to be alone.

"Soon, don't worry," Luka replied with a shrug. "I just need a couple of days."

"Where will you go?"

Luka looked away. "I honestly don't know."

"Well, I'd avoid the big cities if I were you," Graham advised him. "I've heard that the Midnight Hunters have been growing in strength and numbers lately. Probably not a good time to **get on their bad side**, if you know what I mean."

scoundrel	Halunke, Schurke (veraltet)
deliberately	absichtlich
soberly	nüchtern, vernünftig
to get on sb.'s bad side	sich jds. Unmut zuziehen

Luka was suddenly still and silent, his expression **inscrutable**.

"Well, it's never a good time to get on their bad side, if you remember," Graham continued.

"I remember," Luka replied darkly.

His eyes had narrowed with hatred and deep, angry lines were showing on his face.

"I remember very well indeed."

Übung 37: Multiple choice. Kreuzen Sie jeweils die richtige Variante an!

1. a) ☐ Graham had not read the papers before bringing them home.

   b) ☐ Graham had read the newspapers quite thoroughly before Luka got a chance to see them.

2. a) ☐ Luka knew that Graham liked to be alone, so he was not expecting to be made to feel at home.

   b) ☐ Luka was disappointed by Graham's hostile welcome.

3. a) ☐ Graham advised Luka that big cities could be dangerous.

   b) ☐ Graham did not give Luka advice about where to go next.

4. a) ☐ Luka found Graham's use of the old-fashioned word "scoundrel" irritating.

   b) ☐ Luka did not mind it this time.

The **screeching** of cars and the loud sounds of the crowd **assaulted** Luka's hearing. The city was a shock of noise, motion and powerful smells to his **heightened** senses; it was too much to take in at once.

He had promised himself that he would never return to these streets. The London that he remembered was a **gutter**, and he had decided over a century ago to stick to the fresh air and fresh blood of the countryside. But in all the chaos, there was something beautiful and pure that had drawn him back. He could sense her now, a dim light in the tumult of the city, burning just bright enough for him to follow: Alison.

inscrutable	unergründlich
screeching	(Bremsen-)Quietschen
to assault	überfallen, ein-stürmen auf
heightened	gesteigert, ver-stärkt
gutter	Drecksloch, Gosse

There had still been nothing in the newspapers. If there was even a chance that she had kept his secret deliberately, he needed to know how she felt. He wished that he could stop himself from hoping that her silence was due to her feelings for him – the same feelings which he had for her – but the foolish hope would not leave him.

The streets were shining with recent rain, but the smell [i] that rose up from them was of something else. To Luka's sharp sense of smell, it was an urban cacophony of scent [i], containing hundreds, thousands, of different tones within it. Smoke, sweat, perfume, cheap takeaway

> **Smell** oder **scent**?
> Beide Substantive bezeichnen Gerüche, wobei **smell** eher auch unangenehmer Gestank bedeutet, während **scent** v. a. Duft und, im britischen Englisch, Parfüm meint. Zudem bedeutet scent auch (Duft-)Fährte, **to scent** somit u. a. wittern.

food, petrol. And coming from the crowds that pushed past him on all sides, the smell of every flavour of blood. A city such as this was a meat market for a vampire.

But for Luka, who was used to the silent moors, it was also an onslaught. The city's noise violently pounded through his head. Sights, sounds and smells called for his attention from every side, drowning out the faint sense of Alison's presence.

Still, he continued through the crowds and the noise. Luka could well remember why he had left this urban landscape behind him. Of course, London had been very different when he had last known it: kings and queens had been and gone since then; whole neighbourhoods had been knocked down and new ones, of steel and glass, had been built in their place. Every human who had lived in those times was now dead. But, he reflected, it was not London's human inhabitants that he had to worry about.

He could still remember his very first sight of the place in the late 19th century. Arriving by boat in the crowded, stinking waters of the Thames, he had seen the rats scurry down the ropes as soon as they reached land. They quickly ran off into the night, along the dirty streets. The slums were piled one on top of another and the workhouse stood high above the roads with an imposing presence. In the distance, St Paul's Cathedral stood out on the horizon. The air was heavy and foul-smelling, and the streetlights did not relieve the darkness that crept over the urban chaos. Luka's thoughts turned from the memory. He had lost Alison's presence among the many voices of the city. He turned around as though searching for her, but still the tumult drowned her out. Luka put his hands to his head: he had come so far for

onslaught	Attacke, Ansturm
to scurry	huschen
to pile	stapeln
workhouse	Armenhaus
imposing	eindrucksvoll, imposant
foul-smelling	übel riechend
grinding	zermürbend
to lurk	lauern

this faint hope, for a promise that was never made. But he had no choice, he simply had to find her.

Übung 38: Unscramble. Lesen Sie weiter und bilden Sie Wörter aus dem Buchstabenchaos!

Alison yawned and **1. denchag** _____

the channel. Jess had gone out with some friends, but

Alison did not feel like doing anything in **2. cartiularp**

_____. The week at work had passed in a

colourless, grinding blur of **3. dobremo** _____.

Even things that she normally **4. jondeye** _____,

like going out for a drink with her colleagues, had not had

their **5. aulus** _____ effect on her.

She flicked through several different programmes until suddenly something made her pause. It was a show that she had seen a few times before and never thought anything of until now: Vampire Killers. She wondered whether its makers knew that their subject was not fiction, but real. A chill passed through her, and she quickly changed the channel.

The world seemed so different now that she knew that she shared it with vampires. There were so many reminders that she often wondered what could be lurking outside in the darkness of the night. Luka had not mentioned whether there were any of his kind in London, or how many there might be in Britain.

Over the last few days, Alison had thought of so many questions that she wished she had asked him before she left his lonely house in the Highlands. But there were also questions for herself that she could not answer: why had she still not told anyone about Luka? What made her want to protect him? And why, why on earth, did she still feel a longing for him that obeyed no logic or reason?

Perhaps she would tell Jess tonight. Even if she did not believe her, just saying the words out loud would surely be better than keeping them chained up in her heart. This silence was unbearable.

to obey	gehorchen, folgen
to chain (up)	festketten
unbearable	unerträglich
delicate	zerbrechlich, fein

Alison switched off the television and walked to her bedroom window. It was a cold night, but she opened the window and reached outside with her hands, just to feel something physical and real. To her surprise, a tiny, icy snowflake dropped into her hand. She watched it melt on her pale palm, then let her eyes return to the scene outside. A few white dots were falling through the sky, so delicate and faint, and so tiny in so much blackness.

Übung 39: Adjectives. Schreiben Sie die passenden Adjektive zu den Substantiven auf!

1. logic _____

2. silence _____

3. ice _____

4. protection _____

Alison stayed by the window and watched the snow fall. She was looking down at the garden, watching the snowflakes vanish as they hit the ground below, when suddenly she noticed a figure approaching. She had almost no time to feel afraid as it jumped up like no human could have done and climbed the side of her house in a split second. A face stared straight at her.

She felt her heart pounding violently in her chest and heard her own gasping breath break the silence. But no sooner had panic **kicked in** than she recognized the darkly handsome face at her window. She stepped back in shock and put her hand to her mouth.

"How did you find me?" she whispered before finding her voice. More loudly, she continued: "And how did you do *that*?"

"I'm a vampire," Luka answered playfully.

Alison let out a small, nervous laugh.

"I sensed you," Luka continued. "I followed your presence and found you here. I'm… I'm sorry if I scared you."

Only now did he seem to be realizing the strangeness of this **courtship**.

"Scared isn't the word! You *terrified* me, Luka! I'm still shaking now!" Alison's heart was pounding, but the fear was beginning **to give way to** other emotions. She was shocked to see him again, then she felt a familiar mixture of confusion and attraction.

"Do I need to invite you in?"

Luka looked momentarily confused. "What? Oh, for me to be able to enter? No, that's just another **myth**." As if to prove it, he climbed through the window without a sound.

⚡ to kick in	einsetzen, Wirkung entfalten
courtship	(Liebes-)Werben
to give way to	weichen
myth	Mythos, Gerücht

"I hope I haven't done the wrong thing by coming here and scaring you like this," he said. "I know it must seem crazy. I just… I need to know something. If I'm acting on a foolish hope, then I will leave you alone and I'll never bother you again. I promise. But the tiny, insane possibility that you might feel the same way as I do has been tearing me apart for days… Tell me, why didn't you go to the police or the newspapers and tell them about me?"

"I… I don't know," Alison stuttered.

She had wondered about this many times, too, and now her feelings were further confused by the words he had just spoken. Surely this was madness. There could be no future for a relationship between a human and a vampire.

A thought that had been bothering Alison suddenly came to the front of her mind. "You didn't use some kind of mind trick to keep me silent, then?"

Luka's forehead wrinkled, and he shook his head. "I didn't do anything to your mind that night. And I never will, I promise."

Alison's eyes were large and honest, and when she turned to look at him they were full of emotion.

"Then, I suppose, I just couldn't stand to put you in danger. I feel too much for you. Maybe I'm crazy, too, but I can't hide from what's in my heart. I want to be with you."

The old shadows of Luka's expression seemed to fade as his face filled with emotions that were unfamiliar to him: disbelief, happiness and warmth.

"I feel the same. I tried to forget about you, but I just couldn't."

Luka took her gently in his strong arms. She stiffened for a moment, then let her feelings take over: they were too strong for her to ignore any longer. She put her arms around him and kissed his neck softly, then, moving her mouth to his, she began to press harder. Her teeth grazed his lips and quiet moans escaped her lips. He picked her up effortlessly and carried her to the bed.

Alison's body shuddered with desire; she paid no attention to the snowflakes that blew in through the open window. Alison clasped Luka's hand and ex-

| to clasp | umklammern |
| to ripple | sich kräuseln, wogen |

citedly pulled him onwards into the night. An hour before, back in her home, they had talked about his memories of London, which were so different to her own experiences of the capital. There were so many things she wanted to show him to change his mind about the place.

And perhaps, if she was able to make him see London's beauty, he might come to think that this was a city he could eventually call home. They had not spoken about the future, but Alison could not help but begin to imagine their lives together.

Übung 40: Odd one out. Unterstreichen Sie das nicht in die Reihe passende Wort!

1. courtship | date | vacation | flirtation
2. myth | tale | evidence | legend
3. promise | vow | guarantee | attempt
4. tear | mend | fracture | rip

Eventually, they reached the point that she had in mind. She placed her hands on the cool metal wall of the bridge and looked out across the Thames to where the moon's reflection gently rippled. St Paul's Cathedral was brightly lit up on the other side of the riverbank, and in the other direction Big Ben stood tall, looking out over the city.

"I remember this view," Luka whispered into her ear.

He held her from behind with his face close to hers.

"Don't you think it's beautiful?" she asked.

Luka imagined the rats leaving his boat, and the smell of the slums wafting across the dark waters of the Thames.

"So much more beautiful than when I last saw it," he told her.

"I'm sure everything has changed since then," Alison said as if reading his mind. "There are no slums here now, and no work-houses. There are great places everywhere, where people eat, drink and enjoy themselves. I'm going to show you my London tonight. Come with me."

5  Daybreak

Dawn was approaching. The couple had wandered through the city for several hours, stopping in bars and in all of Alison's favourite hidden spots. They had just been for a walk in Hyde Park beneath the thin moon. Even in the dark, Luka had been surprised by the beauty of the place. Alison sensed that he was starting to see London with fresh eyes.

Finally, they were approaching home. Alison yawned and leant on Luka's shoulder for support as they walked on. Everything was quiet except for the sound of their footsteps along the empty road. "I'm so sleepy," she said, yawning again. "I don't know how I'm going to keep up with your lifestyle."

He took her hand and kissed it, then continued to hold it as they walked together.

"I can adapt to yours," Luka said. "I can stay awake through the day; I just can't do much outside."

> **To adapt (oneself) to** bedeutet sich anpassen an, das Reflexivpronomen kann dabei im Englischen entfallen.

"You could paint!" Alison suggested excitedly. "You won't need to work as a cleaner here – you can sell your work instead. I know of all sorts of shops that would be interested. And believe me, you won't need to worry about nosy neighbours. Nobody pays the least bit of attention to their neighbours here."

"Perhaps, perhaps," Luka said with a slight smile.

He was beginning to get used to the idea of life in London. Life with Alison, he thought happily.

Alison looked up at his rugged face and smiled. She felt so happy. Nothing else in the world seemed to matter, she thought to herself **contentedly**.

In the next second, a violent blow hit the back of her head and she heard a sound coming from above. Instinctively Alison reached around to shield herself, but someone, something, caught her arm and twisted it behind her back, where her other arm was also trapped. She screamed out **in agony**. Any movement she made caused pain to shoot down her back, but she had to see who had attacked her and what had happened to Luka.

Twisting her neck to look behind her, she saw the fangs that she had feared. The rest was a blur. And then she recognized Luka, already metres away and struggling furiously against four vampires. They were dragging him further away from her with unnatural force and speed. His muscles were **taut** and his veins **bulging**: fighting, he looked like a **fierce** animal, but there were too many of them hunting him.

"Luka!" she called out.

He looked around, and for a moment their eyes met, **mirroring** each other's expressions of angry helplessness. Then Luka's gaze shifted to her attacker and his face filled with rage. He appeared to recognize the vampire. Murderous anger blazed through his eyes, which had turned a **fiery** silver. Its

contentedly	stillvergnügt, zufrieden
in agony	vor Schmerzen
taut	angespannt
to bulge	hervortreten
fierce	wild, bedrohlich
to mirror	widerspiegeln
fiery	feurig, glühend

power gave him the strength to throw off three vampires and run towards Alison, but the remaining vampire grabbed hold of him and held him tight. It was long enough for the others to hurry back around him and finally drag him to the ground.

Alison had to look away. She could not bear to see him being beaten from all sides like this.

Unexpectedly, Alison was jolted backwards by a sudden movement. She still had not seen who was attacking her, but whoever it was was pulling her backwards very fast. Her arms felt as if they were being ripped off from behind. She lost one of her shoes after its heel caught on a hole in the pavement.

Alison did not know where she was being taken: all she could see was the scenery in front of her getting further away, then a huge metal gate and a door in what looked like a warehouse. She was dragged through the door and thrown to the hard ground.

Alison heard the sound of a switch. Everything was suddenly flooded with cold fluorescent light. She had no time to take in her surroundings: her eyes searched immediately for the figure who had brought her here, and who was now locking the door with its back turned.

Without concentrating on the pain, she picked herself up from the floor and ran forward with her arms raised to strike her attacker.

"I wouldn't bother," a cold male voice said sharply.

The man did not even turn around, but at a frightening speed he hit her forcefully around the jaw, knocking her to the floor once again. Alison let out a wounded sound as she picked herself up and tasted the blood in her mouth. She heard the metallic clunk of the door locking. The sound had a finality to it that filled her with fear.

"I hope you've learnt your lesson, silly child. Because the next time you try anything like that your punishment will be much, much worse."

With those words, the man finally turned around. He had straight, ice-white hair that reached to below his shoulders, and a thin, callous face. Alison was taken aback: he looked like a cold, cruel angel.

"Wh... What do you want?" she managed to say, in a voice that she barely recognized.

to jolt	reißen, schleudern
warehouse	Lagerhalle
jaw	Kiefer
clunk	(dumpfes) Krachen
finality	Endgültigkeit
callous	hart, kaltschnäuzig
to be taken aback	schockiert sein
nonchalantly	lässig

"Oh, don't ask stupid questions," he responded nonchalantly. "Try again."

Alison's eyes narrowed in anger.

"Who are you, and what are you going to do to me?" she spat.

"My name is Stephan, and I have a few things in mind for you. But why spoil the surprise?"

"Where's Luka? Who's taken him?"

"Don't worry your little head, he's not far away," her attacker replied. "And he's in good company... He's with some old friends, in fact. But as for you, I'm afraid I'm going to have to leave you all on your own."

His taunting tone made Alison shake with rage, but even as he turned to leave she knew that there was nothing she could do. Her speed and strength would be no match for him.

Übung 42: Synonyms. Finden Sie im vorhergehenden Textabschnitt die Synonyme der folgenden Wörter!

1. to ruin _____

2. cold-hearted _____

3. indifferently _____

4. powerfully _____

Stephan left the room, locking the door again behind him, and Alison was alone. Her short, gasping breaths echoed through the empty room. Now that the initial shock was wearing off, panic had taken its place. Frantically she looked around the room for something that she could use to defend herself, but there was nothing. And what defence could there be against a vampire, anyway?

The room was completely barren. It looked as if it had once been used for some industrial purpose; the one small window was boarded up with thick wooden panels that were screwed into place. She had no hope of removing them. The only other thing in the room was a metal pipe that ran from one end of the far wall to the other. It must have been part of the heating system, though it was certainly not in use now. Alison shivered: her ripped coat did not offer enough protection against the bitter cold.

frantically	hektisch, verzweifelt
panel	Platte
to screw	schrauben
to crumble	zerbröseln
undercurrent	Unterton

Stephan's words had told her little about what danger Luka might be in, and her mind was filled with panic. Seeing him attacked so viciously had been unbearable. What did they want? She remembered the look of hatred in his eyes when he recognized Stephan carrying her away. What was going on?

Angrily, she picked up her remaining shoe, which had fallen off when she was thrown to the ground, and threw it hard at the wall in frustration. To her surprise, the sound that it made when it hit the pipe was not as hard and metallic as she would have expected.

Alison searched with her hands from one end of the pipe to the other. As the sound had suggested, parts of it had rusted away to nothing. She pushed her fingers through a hole in the top of the pipe, where the rusty metal had grown so soft that it crumbled at her touch. She pulled back instinctively: the edge was still sharp.

Übung 43: Translation. Lesen Sie weiter und übersetzen Sie den Textabschnitt ins Deutsche!

Carefully, she pulled at the rusty metal that screwed the pipe to the wall. Yes, she thought, yes, she could use this. It took all her strength, but she finally pulled away a piece of pipe and hid it behind her back in case Stephan returned.

_____

_____

_____

_____

_____

The room fell silent when Stephan entered. The others showed him their respect, but he spoke to only one person.

"I bet you were hoping you'd never see *me* again," Stephan said, his words lifted by an undercurrent of laughter.

Luka's violent shouts were **muffled** beneath the **gag** that they had tied around his mouth. He was chained to the wall, and every muscle was **straining** to get free and to hurt Stephan in the worst possible way. "Oh dear," Stephan said nonchalantly as he turned to his audience. There were more vampires here now, and the similarity of their style

to muffle	dämpfen, ersticken
gag	Knebel
to strain	(sich) spannen, anstrengen
to pat	klopfen, tätscheln
clattering	klappernd, rasselnd
to bellow	brüllen, lauthals schreien
to whine	jammern, quengeln
stake	Pflock

of dress made it clear that they were all members of the same gang. Only Stephan was dressed differently; he was wearing an old-fashioned jacket and trousers with tall, black boots. The others, in their leather and denim, were giving him all their attention.

"I don't think my old friend is very pleased to see me, after all!" Stephan concluded, his voice rippling with amusement.

He **patted** his prisoner on the shoulder, which sent Luka into even more of a rage. He was straining wildly against the chains, and their **clattering** metal sound echoed through the room. He was shouting, but the words did not escape the gag.

Luka cupped his hand to his ear, pretending to be deaf.

"What's that, old boy?" he asked.

With that he removed the gag from Luka's face and an angry stream of words could finally escape.

"How dare you involve Alison in this!" Luka **bellowed**. "This is between you and me! If you weren't such a coward, you'd let us finish this between ourselves, and God knows I would *kill* you!"

"Oh come, now, don't be so melodramatic!" Stephan responded. "If you don't stop **whining**, I will just kill you straight away!"

Stephan's playful tone suddenly turned to ice-cold hatred and his face twisted with cruelty. He pulled a **stake** from the inside of his jacket and brought it down violently towards Luka's chest. The motion of his arm stopped an instant before the stake met with flesh.

Then Stephan laughed again.

"But where would be the fun in that?"

The other vampires howled with laughter.

"Kill me if you have to, Stephan, but don't hurt the girl," Luka said. His body was suddenly calm and still, and his tone was firm.

Now it was Stephan's turn to let out a loud, hysterical laugh. He held his sides and shook with laughter, almost choking on the sound. The rest of the gang began to join in nervously.

"Enough!" Stephan suddenly cried out to silence them.

Then he brought his face within centimetres of Luka's and stared straight at him. His eyes were pools of cold silver fire, and his snarling lips exposed a vicious set of shining white fangs.

Übung 44: Match-up. Verbinden Sie die Satzanfänge mit der passenden Fortsetzung!

1. ☐ It was clear that the vampires were a gang...

2. ☐ The sound of clattering metal...

3. ☐ Stephan taunted Luka...

4. ☐ When the gag was removed, Luka's words...

a) echoed around the room.

b) could finally be heard.

c) because of their similar style of dress.

d) by making jokes and patting him on the shoulder.

"I sensed your stink as soon as you set foot in London, Luka. But a girl with you? That was a surprise. Did you really think that you could take a human lover and live happily ever after? Don't you think the three-hundred-year age gap could have become a tiny, little problem at some point?"

Finally, one of the watching vampires spoke up.

"It's wrong, that's what it is!" squawked the voice of a thin, black-haired woman with a deep scar across her face.

"Unnatural!" agreed another.

"What it is is dangerous!" Stephan shouted above them, and all eyes returned to him once again.

age gap	Altersunter-schied
glint	Funkeln
to convulse	zucken, ver-krampfen
fury	Wut, Zorn
captor	Kidnapper

"How dare you tell a human what you are!" he screamed at Luka. "Don't you know that it could destroy us all? These days all it takes is for one newspaper to find out, and the story can cross the globe in less than a day!"

"She hasn't told anyone," Luka argued, but he knew too well that Stephan was correct.

"And she won't. Don't worry, she won't!"

An evil glint flashed in Stephan's eye, and Luka convulsed with wild fury, straining against the heavy chains that held him. His eyes were murderous.

"Don't you touch her!" he bellowed.

"Funny, really. I never took you for the naive type. Of course she has to die," Stephan said.

His tone had the casual unimportance with which someone might discuss the weather.

"No!" Luka roared. "Let me out of these chains!"

He focused his eyes firmly on his captor. "I made you Stephan, and I will destroy you, too!"

Übung 45: Idiomatic expressions. Ergänzen Sie die Wendungen!

side   back   after   floodgates   cupped   aback

1. Alison was taken _____ by Stephan's appearance.

2. "Be careful: you don't want to get on their bad _____."

3. Once you've opened the _____, it's hard to stop.

4. Stephan _____ his hand to his hear, pretending to be deaf.

5. My boss is always bothering me. I wish he would get off my _____.

6. A human and a vampire could never live happily ever _____.

A number of the other vampires stepped back and gasped. There was a short silence, during which one vampire was rubbing his hands together excitably and others were smiling, their eyes wide open and curious.

"Ah, yes. For those of you who aren't aware, there is a bit of history between myself and my dear friend here," Stephan began.

Luka heard a slight **waver** in his voice now.

"The history is simple," Luka interrupted, staring straight into Stephan's callous face. "I created you, and not one year later you **framed** me for killing Joanna, the leader of the Midnight Hunters. You wanted to make sure that they came after me with the full force of their fury. I was lucky to escape with my life."

waver	Zögern, Schwanken
to frame sb.	jmd. etw. anhängen
vulture	Geier
traitor	Verräter

Luka looked around the room at the other vampires, who were waiting like **vultures** for more revelations to spill from his mouth. Some, the older ones [i] he assumed, seemed to show recognition when he mentioned Joanna's name. He looked closer into their faces. Yes... he knew them from somewhere. Then the realization hit him with sudden force.

"It all makes sense now. I see you've made your own rival gang here, Stephan, and I recognize some of them... they're old members of

One als Stützwort

Soll im Englischen ein Substantiv im Satz nicht wiederholt werden, muss das zugehörige Adjektiv mit dem Stützwort **one** (Singular) oder **ones** (Plural) ergänzt werden: "the older Midnight Hunters" wird zu "the older ones".

the Midnight Hunters. No wonder you wanted Joanna out of the way! You thought you could steal her power, didn't you? All you needed was someone to frame for her death, and the rest was easy!"

The other vampires were coming closer now.

"You mean, *you* killed Joanna?" one of them shouted, pointing at his leader with a shaking hand. His face was filled with disgust.

"Don't believe this **traitor**!" Stephan cried out, shaking with rage. "Honestly, I don't know where I found such a dumb, useless gang! I told you earlier tonight that he would try to spread his lies the moment we let him speak."

Übung 46: Prepositions. Lesen Sie weiter und vervollständigen Sie den Text mit den folgenden Präpositionen!

in   at   by   by   of   over

He raised his voice and looked around the room **1.** _____

the faces **2.** _____ every one of his followers.

"This is the one who killed the great Joanna van den Driessche

3. _____ locking her **4.** _____ a curtainless prison to

die **5.** _____ the sun's fire! Of course he lies! And he must

be destroyed!"

Triumphantly, Stephan put the gag back **6.** _____ Luka's

mouth and the prisoner's cries were muffled once again.

Alison was pressed against the wall with the pipe gripped tightly between her cold hands. She was waiting only a few centimetres from the door so that she would be able to leap forward and stake whoever entered the room as soon as it opened. She was ready, and full of adrenaline. Every thought and all of her senses were concentrated on the task ahead of her.

After what felt like a long wait, the door swung open, and Stephan's white-blond hair flashed in the corner of her eye. As quickly as she could, she swung forwards with the pipe and brought it down violently towards his heart.

"Stupid girl!" Stephan hissed.

He easily caught her wrist with a grip that felt like steel, and held it in front of him. The stake was so close to its target, but he had her arm locked in his grip. She was shaking and her attempts to struggle were useless.

"What did I tell you about learning your lesson?" Stephan roared. "I warned you!"

He forced Alison forward and shut the heavy door behind them. Alison noticed helplessly that he had not locked it, but knew she could never reach it in time.

The vampire leapt up and pushed her downwards onto the hard floor. Her weapon fell from her hand and clattered in the far corner of the room. Stephan landed on top of her, bringing his fangs towards her neck in sickening slow motion.

target	Ziel
searing	schneidend, brennend
to go limp	erschlaffen, erledigt sein
consumed by anger	von (unbändigem) Zorn erfüllt
drenched	durchtränkt

Alison screamed and shook her head wildly, but the vampire's weight and strength were pinning her to the ground. Suddenly a searing pain ripped through her. Stephan lifted his head back up and she saw her own bright red blood smeared across his face. He had ripped her open, she realized with horror. The hot liquid was pouring down her neck as he drank from her.

She could not bring herself to believe the scene that was playing out all around her. She noticed the small details – the drops falling onto her face, pouring down from the pearly daggers of his fangs – as though they were happening to someone else. This could not be her death, not really, she thought stupidly. She was beginning to feel weak from blood loss and was struggling to stay conscious.

Suddenly, the door burst open and something knocked the feeding creature off her. Shapes were moving through her blurred vision, but everything quickly grew dark.

Übung 47: Synonyms. Verbinden Sie die Synonyme!

1. ☐ searing   **a)** vulnerable

2. ☐ grip   **b)** bang

3. ☐ helpless   **c)** burning

4. ☐ clatter   **d)** grasp

Rage pounded through Luka's heart. He struck Stephan with his broken chains, then hit him again and again with every last bit of his hatred and anger until he stopped struggling and finally went limp.
In the room that he had left, Luka could hear the noise of the gang fighting between themselves.

After Stephan had gone, Kieran, a vampire Luka recognized from the old gang, had removed Luka's gag to hear more of what he had to say. Luka had been able to persuade some of them that he was telling the truth about their leader. Many of the vampires who had been part of the Midnight Hunters before Joanna's death seemed to believe him, but some of the younger ones were more loyal to Stephan. The two groups had soon started fighting each other, and Kieran had helped Luka to break free of his chains. In the tumult, Luka had run towards the room that he had seen Stephan enter.

Finally, Luka turned from Stephan's bloodied face and hurried towards Alison. He had been too consumed by anger to look at her properly during the fight, and now... no, no! It couldn't be real! Her eyes were closed and her top was drenched in blood from the violent wound in her neck. She was not moving.

Water was beginning to form in Luka's eyes: he had not cried since his human lifetime, and did not recognize the tears. But he did know the sadness that tore through him. Was he really already too late to save her?

Luka desperately moved to close her wound with his tongue, but he was not able to heal it fully before he was pulled away from her. Two vampires loyal to Stephan were pulling him to his feet.

Consciousness slowly returned to Alison. She saw four indistinct [i] figures moving beside her before her eyes finally focused on a familiar face: Luka. And behind him, Stephan was rising from the ground and, impossibly, his bruised and battered face was changing in front of her eyes. All of his wounds were healing and his bruised skin was quickly regaining its deathly pallor.

> **Indistinct** bedeutet undeutlich oder verschwommen.
> **In-** ist im Englischen neben **un-**, **im-**, **il-**, und **dis-** eine häufige negative Vorsilbe, um Wörter in ihr Gegenteil zu verkehren:
> incredible — unglaublich
> inability — Unfähigkeit

Two vampires who she did not recognize were holding Luka back as Stephan approached him with an evil glint in his silver eyes, and a look of pure hatred written across his face. Without warning, he struck Luka hard around the jaw. Luka roared and threw off the other two vampires, but Stephan felled him with a kick to the stomach. In the background she could hear violent sounds coming from the other room.

Alison looked on in horror while the three vampires struck Luka as he lay on the ground. Tears were flooding her eyes and sobs choked her. What she saw next was even worse: Stephan shouted at the other two

bruised and battered	grün und blau
pallor	Blässe
to fell sb.	jmd. zu Boden strecken
to dodge	ausweichen

to step back and pulled a stake from his jacket. With an evil grin, he held it up in the air, ready to bring it down on Luka.

Übung 48: Infinitive or continuous? Lesen Sie weiter und fügen Sie die richtige Verbform ein!

There were more of the gang at the doorway now and, with a shock of panic, Alison saw one of them **1.** look _____ directly at her, **2.** snarl _____ and licking its cracked, grey lips hungrily. She looked back at Luka: he had noticed the other vampires **3.** appear _____ in the doorway, too. Some of them were **4.** fight _____ each other still, but others were about to **5.** burst _____ into the room.

Time seemed to stand still. Alison saw, over what seemed like minutes, Luka leap up and make a sudden movement towards the boarded-up window. With all his strength, he smashed open the wooden panels and let the rays of the early morning sun burst into the room. Stephan brought down the stake into empty air.

The other vampires hissed and hurried back into the other room; only Stephan remained to finish the job. But his powers were dramatically weakened: his arm trembled as he gripped the stake and stabbed it clumsily. His expression was wild, and he was stabbing desperately in any direction. But each time the stake missed its target. Then it got caught in the door as Luka dodged another blow, and Stephan struggled to pull it out from the wood. The vampire was sluggish and looked extremely tired. Finally, he pulled out the stake, but it fell from his grip and clattered noisily on the floor.

to sag	nachgeben, schlaff werden
to disintegrate	sich zersetzen, sich auflösen
heap	Haufen
to stumble	stolpern
glare	gleißendes Licht
to clutch	umklammern

Frantically, Alison tried to get up and reach the stake, but she was still hopelessly weak. She cried out with frustration. It was so close!

On the other side of the room, Luka was still struggling against Stephan's frenzied attacks.

Alison gathered every last bit of strength she had and dragged herself across the floor. Finally, she was able to grasp the weapon.

"Luka!" she called out and threw it to him.

He caught it and rammed it straight into Stephan's heart. Before he could even scream, his body sagged and started to disintegrate.

There was no time to waste in celebration. Luka ran to Alison and licked at her wound to heal it completely.

"Are you all right?" he asked as he helped her back onto her feet.

He was attempting to find cover from the light that was pouring in through the broken window. Standing up, Alison put her fingers to her throat to feel her skin. It was smooth and unharmed.

"I feel faint, but I'll be okay. What about you?"

"I can't last too long in this light..."

Luka's expression was brave, but she could tell that he was becoming weak. She remembered the evil snarls of the vampire in the doorway and the violent gang that was just metres away.

"We can't go back in there," she said.

Luka shuddered. He could already feel the scorching sun on his skin; outside it would be a thousand times worse. But Alison was right: they had to leave. Immediately.

Squinting in the brightening sunshine, Luka tried the handle of the main door, but it was locked. Alison fumbled for the key in Stephan's trousers, which lay in a heap where his body had disintegrated. She found it and quickly put the key in the lock.

Arm in arm, they stumbled out together into the glare of the morning sun.

Luka felt the searing sensation of light on his skin. He knew that it would only be a few minutes before the agony was too much to bear.

Alison lifted her coat over him to cover his head and shoulders.

"Can you make it to my house?" she asked frantically.

"Is it far?" Luka asked. He did not know the way.

"Ten minutes, if we run."

"Yes, I'll be fine," Luka said, but he was already stumbling.

He had clearly been weakened by the fight and the morning sunlight.

"Come with me," she instructed as she led him towards safety.

Whether it was due to the healing of her wounds, the fresh air, or the adrenaline, Alison no longer felt weak or frightened. She knew exactly what she needed to do.

London was awakening around them. The roads were no longer empty and people were beginning to walk the streets. Clutching the coat above him, Luka felt the familiar fear of being discovered, but that was the least of his worries now. His red hands were turning raw and beginning to blister.

Finally the industrial landscape gave way to the residential area where Alison lived. Luka glimpsed the bare trees and the tidy rows of houses from under the black coat. His hands were in agony, and, even with its cover, his face was beginning to feel the hot fire of the sun. Parts of his clothes had been ripped in the fight and rays of light were stabbing at the skin beneath them.

"We're not far away now," Alison said. Her voice was thin and worried.

Luka struggled on. He could not help but look behind him, but thankfully nobody was following them.

After what seemed like hours of desperate running, Alison pushed her key into the door and they ran

to blister	Blasen werfen
residential area	Wohngegend
to snore	schnarchen
singed	angesengt, ver-brannt
tear	*hier:* Riss
to sting	brennen
solitude	Einsamkeit

inside. She took him straight upstairs, past the bedroom where Jess lay snoring after her night out, and into her own room. She pulled down the shutters and they collapsed onto the bed.

Alison looked around at the singed vampire beside her and her eyes widened with shock. Luka's hands were blistered and black, his face red, and the parts of his body that had been exposed by the tears in his clothes were raw and burned. She put her hand to her mouth.

"Why did you break open the window?" she asked. "It could have killed you as well as your enemies!"

"I had to make sure that you were safe," Luka said as he slumped back on her bed. "That was all that mattered."

"What about *you*?" Tears were stinging Alison's eyes.

"I've put you into enough danger already," he sighed and closed his eyes. "I'm so sorry, Alison. I knew that taking you into my darkness would only cause you pain."

Alison put her hand to his lips. "No, no, that isn't what you've done! I... I can't explain it, Luka, but when I'm with you, I feel alive. I just know that when I'm by your side, I'm exactly where I'm meant to be."

"I feel the same," Luka told her softly. "I was so scared that I'd lost you. I could never have lived with myself if you'd been harmed."

Alison looked again at Luka's burnt skin. She remembered the way that Stephan's injuries had healed themselves before her eyes.

"Will these burns heal?"

Luka shook his head. "Not quickly; I'm too weak. I won't be able to heal until my strength returns."

"What will it take for you to get your strength back?" Alison asked, but she had already guessed the answer.

Luka opened his mouth as if to speak, then seemed to change his mind.

"Luka, I know what you need," Alison said matter-of-factly, determined not to let herself get emotional about the matter. "How much?"

"Just a little," he eventually replied. "But you can't, Alison. You're too weak. Please, I don't want your blood."

"You may not want it, but you need it. Look at yourself."

She pointed at his ruined hands. "I want you to have it."

"Are you sure?"

"Completely."

Luka looked overwhelmed. It meant so much to him that she was offering herself in this way. He could feel a love begin to stir in him that broke through the solitude of three dark centuries.

"Tell me if it hurts and I'll stop," he said gently.

Übung 50: Vocabulary quiz. Schreiben Sie die passenden Begriffe auf und enträtseln Sie das Lösungswort!

1. Vampire's teeth ☐ _ _ _ _
2. A synonym for injury _ ☐ _ _ _
3. Someone who gives blood _ _ _ _ ☐
4. A red swelling on one's skin _ _ _ _ _ ☐ _
5. The opposite of hell _ _ _ ☐ _ _
6. A weapon used to kill vampires _ _ _ _ ☐
7. Alison's favourite kind of film _ _ ☐ _ _ _

Lösung: ☐ ☐ ☐ ☐ ☐ ☐ ☐

Alison felt a prickle of fear, but exposed her neck to him as casually as she could manage. Her trembling hands contradicted the bold-ness of the gesture.

Luka gently approached the pale skin of Alison's neck. She could imagine his fangs extending like the claws of a cat, but did not want to look. Suddenly, she felt the momentary pain of the bite. For a brief second the pain was mixed with pleasure, and then an intense sensation overwhelmed her.

Just as Luka had said, it was like an incredibly sensual kiss, one that seemed to reach beyond her body and mind into something com-pletely new. She wanted to swim in that sensation forever, but be-fore she knew it, it was over. She opened her eyes, and there was

Luka's handsome face staring at her lovingly. His skin was already beginning to heal, regaining its pale beauty. The wounds on his hands were closing in front of her very eyes.

"You know," she said, smiling, "I think I could get used to this."

Luka's eyes suddenly **glazed over** with sadness. He turned away for a moment and began to speak.

"I could, too. But I don't know how we can stay together. Stephan's gang could come after us at any time. My life's too dangerous to share with you, especially here."

Alison breathed in deeply.

"Then we'll leave London."

"But it's your home... your life is here... your job," Luka said, utterly shocked.

boldness	Kühnheit
to glaze over	glasig werden
to recall	*hier:* erinnern an

"I *hate* my job," Alison laughed. "And I know this is all very sudden, but after what we've been through together... I'm sure, more sure than I've ever been about anything, that I want you in my life. The last thing I would be able to do is go back to normality and forget about you. I just couldn't do it."

Luka looked completely taken aback. The thought that anybody could feel this way about him was so unexpected that it seemed almost ridiculous. He laughed in surprise at his thoughts. Eventually, he managed to put them into words.

"I can't be without you either, Alison. We'll make this work! We just need to think about where to go... what we'll do for a living..."

Alison put her finger over Luka's mouth. There would be plenty of time to think about all the details later, and besides, she didn't care what they did so long as they were together. She cupped his jaw with one hand and leant in towards him.

He kissed her hungrily, with a fierce and sensual passion that **recalled** the intense sensation of his bite. Alison let herself be lost in it. There was nothing else that mattered.

Abschlusstest

Übung 1: Questions to the text. Beantworten Sie die Fragen zum Text!

1. How did Alison find out that Luka was a vampire?

_____

_____

2. Why did Luka leave the Highland town where he lived?

_____

_____

3. How did Luka get free from the chains at the warehouse?

_____

_____

4. How did Stephan die?

_____

Übung 2: Unscramble. Bilden Sie sinnvolle Wörter!

1. Alison's `dregarmonth` _____ sometimes worried about her.

2. Luka had lived in `ceyresc` _____ for centuries.

3. Being bitten by a vampire can be a `elplasaurbe` _____ experience.

4. `enisnush` _____ is a danger to Luka.

5. Alison's blood was dripping from the `dalbe` _____ of the knife.

6. Alison had never `tadinfe` _____ before Luka tried to erase her memories.

Übung 3: Idiomatic expressions. Unterstreichen Sie die richtige Variante!

1. She sat `bolt` / `lightning` upright in bed.

2. Finally, Alison `regained` / `rejoined` consciousness.

3. The doctor's analysis `put` / `shed` no light on the problem.

4. Her curiosity `got` / `found` the better of her.

5. In London, Luka `headed` / `heated` straight towards Alison.

Übung 4: Passive voice. Wandeln Sie die Sätze ins Passiv um!

1. Luka killed Stephan.

   _____

2. The boss has cancelled the office party.

   _____

3. Nobody saw the attack outside Fairburn.

   _____

4. Kieran released Luka from the chains.

   _____

Übung 5: Who is described? Ordnen Sie die Charakterisierungen richtig zu!

Alison ☐   Luka ☐   Stephan ☐   Graham ☐   Jess ☐

1. A strong and powerful vampire who falls in love.
2. A vampire who works at a hospital, and who does not like company.
3. A pretty girl who enjoys cooking and baking.
4. A power-hungry vampire with an evil nature.
5. A curious girl who works in telesales but longs for a more exciting life.

Übung 6: Word spiral. Finden Sie die Begriffe in der Wortspirale!

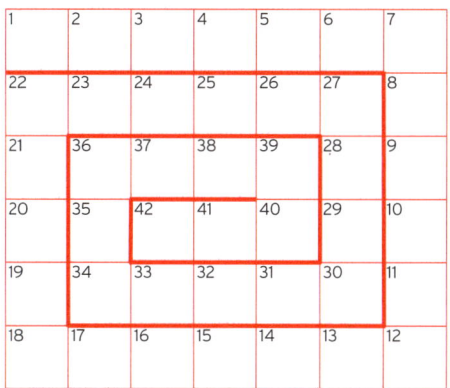

1	2	3	4	5	6	7
22	23	24	25	26	27	8
21	36	37	38	39	28	9
20	35	42	41	40	29	10
19	34	33	32	31	30	11
18	17	16	15	14	13	12

1-9: The coming of night; dusk.

9-18: Solitude, isolation.

18-24: To walk unsteadily or trip.

24-28: Without contents.

28-31: An action showing tiredness.

31-34: A synonym for tidy.

34-40: Someone who betrays someone else.

40-42: A shaft of light.

Übung 7: Odd one out. Unterstreichen Sie das „schwarze Schaf"!

1. ruby   diamond   scarlet   crimson

2. stab   attack   assault   defend

3. expose   glisten   shine   glimmer

4. boldness   courage   cowardliness   bravery

Übung 8: Translation. Übersetzen Sie!

1. Leinwand   _____

2. unstillbar   _____

3. höhnen   _____

4. karg   _____

5. mit leiser Stimme   _____

6. Blutrausch   _____

Übung 9: Fill in the blanks. Ergänzen Sie die Begriffe!

blazed   pounded   extended   fake   drowned out   hiss

rapidly   splattered

1. The vampire's cat-like   pierced the silence.

2. Its fangs   and its eyes   silver.

3. The victim's heartbeat   .

4. Blood   on the ground.

5. The screams were   by the wind.

6. Alison thought that she had been attacked by a madman with   vampire teeth.

Lösungen

Übung 1: **1.** pointed **2.** howl **3.** chill **4.** Highlands

Übung 2: **1.** falsch (Alison is watching an old vampire film.) **2.** falsch (Eve does not want to watch the film.) **3.** richtig **4.** richtig

Übung 3: **1.** people **2.** scarves **3.** buses **4.** bus stops

Übung 4: **1.** grabbed **2.** fangs **3.** neck **4.** attack **5.** scarf **6.** bite

Übung 5: **1.** slowly **2.** heavily **3.** deeply **4.** gently **5.** wildly

Übung 6: **1.** scream **2.** vampire **3.** distant **4.** frown **5.** violent **6.** dangerous **7.** shudder **8.** arrest **Lösung:** midnight

Übung 7: **1.** c **2.** a **3.** d **4.** b **5.** e

Übung 8: **1.** exclaimed **2.** put **3.** held **4.** checked **5.** could

Übung 9: **1.** control **2.** memory **3.** dreadful **4.** bolt upright

Übung 10: **1.** confused **2.** sense **3.** pillow **4.** echo **5.** continued **6.** before

Übung 11: **1.** c **2.** d **3.** e **4.** b **5.** a

Übung 12: **1.** rest **2.** blackout **3.** With these words **4.** coat **5.** opened

Übung 13: **1.** felt, felt **2.** hid, hidden **3.** rang, rung **4.** clung, clung **5.** relieved, relieved

Übung 14:

C	S	T	R	A	N	G	E	R
A	X	K	I	Q	C	D	E	J
F	W	U	N	E	A	S	E	Y
A	A	B	S	I	K	V	X	A
N	T	L	A	S	B	I	P	C
G	T	R	N	B	I	C	H	C
S	A	B	I	T	E	T	R	E
Z	C	W	T	G	R	I	L	N
F	K	A	Y	N	O	M	M	T

Übung 15: **1.** armchair **2.** offer **3.** feelings **4.** captivating **5.** returned **6.** comfortable

Übung 16: **1.** maniac **2.** hometown **3.** remote **4.** checked

Übung 17: **1.** b, e, f **2.** a, c, d

Übung 18: **1.** c **2.** a **3.** b **4.** e **5.** d

Übung 19: kitchen, pull, hand, wrist, lights, glow, firelight

Übung 20: **1.** b **2.** a **3.** c

Übung 21: **1.** boredom **2.** love **3.** despair **4.** protect **5.** dark

Übung 22: **1.** It wouldn't make much difference whether she stayed or left.
2. It's not just that I won't do it – I can't do it.
3. But I'm not going to do anything – I don't hurt people.
4. He wasn't accustomed to feeling pity, but he felt it now.

Übung 23: licked, was, had been expecting, pulled, looked, saw, had been, was, remained, took, showed, said

Übung 24:

1 R	2 E	3 V	4 U	5 L	6 S	7 I
22 E	23 D	24 E	25 S	26 P	27 A	8 O
21 S	36 N	37 I	38 A	39 C	28 I	9 N
20 O	35 A	42 F	41 E	40 H	29 R	10 A
19 P	34 M	33 L	32 A	31 P	30 I	11 R
18 X	17 E	16 P	15 I	14 W	13 O	12 R

Übung 25: **1.** began **2.** everything **3.** erase **4.** let **5.** eyebrow **6.** would

Übung 26: **1.** When new vampires are created, they are like animals with no control over their bloodlust.
2. Luka calls such a human a "donor".
3. A vampire's bite can be a pleasurable experience for the donor.
4. The human must die giving his or her blood to the vampire, then they must feed from the vampire's own blood.

Übung 27: **1.** vampire **2.** scene **3.** Holland **4.** blood **5.** clearly **6.** beautiful

Übung 28: **1.** "Who was the other vampire?" asked Alison.
2. "I can still see her face now," said Luka.
3. "Did you ever see her again?" Alison asked.
4. "The vampire died a long time ago," Luka explained.

Übung 29: **1.** substitute **2.** illuminated **3.** taunted **4.** hissed

Übung 30: **1.** richtig **2.** falsch (He opened up because something takes hold of him whenever Alison is around.) **3.** falsch (Alison has no reason to doubt Luka.) **4.** richtig

Übung 31: **1.** She breathed in its cold freshness.
2. It could not be any less like the Highland village she had left earlier that day.
3. They would not believe her anyway.
4. He was walking towards her.

Übung 32: **1.** good **2.** comfortable **3.** down **4.** agreed **5.** freezing

Übung 33: **1.** c **2.** e **3.** b **4.** d **5.** a

Übung 34: **1.** Hopefully, crazy **2.** deeply **3.** wrong **4.** well

Übung 35:

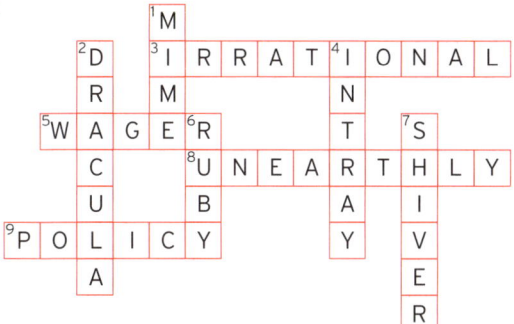

Übung 36: Luka war erleichtert, als Graham zurückkam, ihm die Zeitungen hinwarf und auf seine Reaktion wartete. Schnell durchsuchte Luka eine nach der anderen. Jedes Mal, wenn er eine Zeitung aufschlug, erwartete er, dass Alisons Enthüllung ihm als Schlagzeile schwarz auf weiß entgegenspringen würde.

Übung 37: 1. b 2. a 3. a 4. b

Übung 38: 1. changed 2. particular 3. boredom 4. enjoyed 5. usual

Übung 39: 1. logical 2. silent 3. icy 4. protective

Übung 40: 1. vacation 2. evidence 3. attempt 4. mend

Übung 41: 1. wasn't, Luka's 2. Luka's, Alison's 3. vampires' 4. Luka's, Alison's, attacker's

Übung 42: 1. spoil 2. callous 3. nonchalantly 4. forcefully

Übung 43: Vorsichtig zog sie an dem Metallstück, mit dem das Rohr an der Wand befestigt war. Ja!, dachte sie, Ja, das könnte sie verwenden. All ihre Kraft war nötig, aber schließlich riss sie ein Stück Rohr los und versteckte es hinter ihrem Rücken für den Fall, dass Stephan zurückkäme.

Übung 44: 1. c 2. a 3. d 4. b

Übung 45: 1. aback 2. side 3. floodgates 4. cupped 5. back 6. after

Übung 46: 1. at 2. of 3. by 4. in 5. by 6. over

Übung 47: 1. c 2. d 3. a 4. b

Übung 48: 1. looking 2. snarling 3. appear 4. fighting 5. burst

Übung 49: 1. b 2. c 3. d 4. a

Übung 50: 1. fangs 2. wound 3. donor 4. blister 5. heaven 6. stake 7. horror
Lösung: forever

Abschlusstest

Übung 1: **1.** Alison found out that Luka was a vampire when she cut her hand with a knife. His fangs came out and his eyes turned silver.
2. Luka left because he thought that Alison would tell people that he was a vampire, which would put him in danger.
3. Luka was freed from the chains by Kieran, a former member of the Midnight Hunters.
4. Stephan was killed by Luka, who stabbed him with a stake.

Übung 2: **1.** grandmother **2.** secrecy **3.** pleasurable **4.** Sunshine **5.** blade **6.** fainted

Übung 3: **1.** bolt **2.** regained **3.** shed **4.** got **5.** headed

Übung 4: **1.** Stephan was killed by Luka.
2. The office party has been cancelled by the boss.
3. The attack outside Fairburn was not seen by anyone.
4. Luka was released from the chains by Kieran.

Übung 5: **1.** Luka **2.** Graham **3.** Jess **4.** Stephan **5.** Alison

Übung 6:

1 N	2 I	3 G	4 H	5 T	6 F	7 A
22 B	23 L	24 E	25 M	26 P	27 T	8 L
21 M	36 A	37 I	38 T	39 O	28 Y	9 L
20 U	35 R	42 Y	41 A	40 R	29 A	10 O
19 T	34 T	33 A	32 E	31 N	30 W	11 N
18 S	17 S	16 E	15 N	14 I	13 L	12 E

Übung 7: **1.** diamond **2.** defend **3.** expose **4.** cowardliness

Übung 8: **1.** canvas **2.** ravenous **3.** taunt **4.** barren **5.** in a small voice **6.** bloodlust

Übung 9: **1.** hiss **2.** extended, blazed **3.** pounded rapidly **4.** splattered **5.** drowned out **6.** fake

Glossar

⚡ = umgangssprachlich

to acknowledge	anerkennen, zugeben
to affect	(negativ) beeinflussen
age gap	Altersunterschied
aggravated	genervt, aufgebracht
agonizingly	qualvoll
apprehensive	besorgt
artificial	künstlich
to assault	überfallen, einstürmen auf
barren	karg, öde
to be accustomed to	an etw. gewöhnt sein
bedpan	Bettpfanne
to be glued to the spot	wie angewurzelt dastehen
to bellow	brüllen, lauthals schreien
⚡ to be on sb.'s back	jmd. im Nacken sitzen
to be taken aback	schockiert sein
to be turned (into a vampire)	zum Vampir gemacht werden
blade	Klinge
blank	leer
to blaze	(auf)lodern
bleak	trostlos, kalt
to blister	Blasen werfen
bloodlust	Blutrausch
bloodstain	Blutfleck
blow	Schlag, Hieb
to blur	verschwimmen, undeutlich werden

to board up	mit Brettern zunageln
boldness	Kühnheit
bolt upright	kerzengerade
to bore into sb.'s (eyes)	jmd. mit den Augen durch-bohren
brightly	*hier:* fröhlich
bruised and battered	grün und blau
to bulge	hervortreten
burst	Lodern, Explosion
to burst (burst, burst) from	herausbrechen aus
bus shelter	Wartehäuschen
callous	hart, kaltschnäuzig
camouflage	Tarnbemalung
canvas	Leinwand
captivating	fesselnd, eindringlich
captor	Kidnapper
carnal	körperlich, sinnlich
cautiously	vorsichtig
to chain (up)	festketten
checked	kariert
chef	Koch, Köchin
chill	Kälte
choked	erstickt
cinematic	Kino-
clamouring	Toben
to clasp	umklammern
clattering	klappernd, rasselnd
clichéd	klischeehaft
to cling to sth.	sich (fest)klammern an
cloak	Umhang
clumsily	ungeschickt, unbeholfen
clunk	(dumpfes) Krachen
to clutch	umklammern
cobweb	Spinnweben
to coincide	zusammenfallen, sich über-schneiden mit

to come unstuck	*hier:* aus den Fugen geraten
companionship	Gesellschaft
to compel	zwingen, drängen
to concede	zugeben, einräumen
to conclude	schließen, enden
conflicting	widersprüchlich
consumed by anger	von (unbändigem) Zorn erfüllt
contentedly	stillvergnügt, zufrieden
to convulse	zucken, verkrampfen
courtship	(Liebes-)Werben
to crack	*hier:* krachen
⚡ crap liar	lausige(r) Lügner(in)
to creep (crept, crept)	kriechen
to crumble	zerbröseln
crumpled	verzerrt
to cup	umfassen, die Hände legen um
to curse oneself	sich verfluchen
cutlery	Besteck
dagger	Dolch
deliberately	absichtlich
delicate	zerbrechlich, fein
desolate	trostlos
despair	Verzweiflung
to despise	hassen, verachten
to dig (dug, dug)	bohren, stoßen
dim	matt, schwach
to disintegrate	sich zersetzen, sich auflösen
to dismiss	abtun, aufgeben
distant	*hier:* unnahbar
to dodge	ausweichen
donor	(Blut-)Spender(in)
to doodle	vor sich hin kritzeln
to doubt one's sanity	an seinem Verstand zweifeln
to drag	ziehen, schleifen
to drain	weichen, abfließen
drenched	durchtränkt
to drown out	übertönen

to dwindle	dahinschwinden
eventful	ereignisreich
exhaustion	Erschöpfung
to expose	freilegen, zeigen
to extend	ausstrecken
exterior	Äußeres
to fade	nachlassen, verblassen
faint	schwach
to faint	ohnmächtig werden
fake	unecht
fang	Reißzahn, Vampirzahn
far-fetched	weit hergeholt, an den Haaren herbeigezogen
to feed (fed, fed)	sich ernähren
⚡ fellow	*hier:* Kerl, Typ
to fell sb.	jmd. zu Boden strecken
fierce	wild, bedrohlich; stürmisch
fiery	feurig, glühend
finality	Endgültigkeit
to flash	zucken, blitzen
flatly	ausdruckslos
to flicker	flimmern, flackern
to flinch	(zusammen)zucken
foul-smelling	übel riechend
to fracture	(durch)brechen
to frame sb.	jmd. etw. anhängen
frantically	hektisch, verzweifelt
frenzied	wild, verzerrt
frenzy of light	*hier:* Flammenspiel
to fumble for sth.	nach etw. tasten
fury	Wut, Zorn
gag	Knebel
to gasp	keuchen, nach Luft schnappen
to gather	zusammensuchen
gaze	Blick
to get on sb.'s bad side	sich jds. Unmut zuziehen
to get the better of sb.	mit jmd. durchgehen

to give way to	weichen
glare	gleißendes Licht
to glaze over	glasig werden
to glimpse	flüchtig erblicken
glint	Funkeln
to glisten	glänzen
to go limp	erschlaffen, erledigt sein
gradually	allmählich, nach und nach
to graze	streifen, leicht (an)kratzen
grinding	zermürbend
to growl	knurren
gust	Stoß, Böe
gutter	Drecksloch, Gosse
half-heartedly	halbherzig
halo	Heiligenschein
harm	Schaden
to head straight towards	direkt zusteuern auf
heap	Haufen
heightened	gesteigert, verstärkt
hinge	Scharnier
hint	*hier:* Andeutung, Hauch
hiss	Fauchen
to hold sb. spellbound	jmd. in seinen Bann ziehen
housemate	Mitbewohner(in)
to howl	heulen
to illuminate	erleuchten, erhellen
imaginary	eingebildet, erfunden
to imply	andeuten
imposing	eindrucksvoll, imposant
in agony	vor Schmerzen
in a small voice	mit leiser Stimme
to inhabit	*hier:* durchleben
insanity	Irrsinn
inscrutable	unergründlich
in secrecy	im Verborgenen
insistently	nachdrücklich
in storage	auf Vorrat, auf Lager

intimate	intim, vertraulich
in-tray	Posteingang(sfach)
intrigued	fasziniert
intrusion	*hier:* Fremdkörper
involuntarily	unwillkürlich
irritation	Verärgerung
jaw	Kiefer
to jolt	reißen, schleudern
to justify	rechtfertigen
⚡ to kick in	einsetzen, Wirkung entfalten
light-headed	benommen, schwindelig
to lock	*hier:* sich ineinander bohren
to long	sich sehnen
to lunge	vorpreschen, stürzen
to lurk	lauern
maniac	Verrückte(r)
matter-of-factly	sachlich, nüchtern
to mime	nachahmen
to mirror	widerspiegeln
mischievous	verschmitzt
mist	Nebel
moan	Stöhnen
to muffle	dämpfen, ersticken
myth	Mythos, Gerücht
neat	nett, akkurat
night shift	Nachtschicht
nonchalantly	lässig
nosy	neugierig
to obey	gehorchen, folgen
obsession	Manie, Besessenheit
⚡ Och, aye!	Oh, ja! (schott.)
odd	*hier:* gelegentlich
onslaught	Attacke, Ansturm
to open the floodgates	die Schleusen öffnen
to overwhelm	überwältigen
pallor	Blässe
palm	Handfläche

panel	Platte
paralysis	Lähmung
to pat	klopfen, tätscheln
pawn	Marionette, Spielball
to persist	beharren, insistieren
piercing	durchdringend, stechend
to pile	stapeln
to pin sb. to the ground	jmd. am Boden festhalten
pointed	spitz
pouch	*hier:* Blutkonserve
to pound	schlagen, hämmern
preference	Vorliebe
to prey on	Jagd machen auf
prickle	Kribbeln
⚡ prized	wertvoll, toll
to put one's finger on sth.	etw. genau ausmachen
to radiate	ausstrahlen
raging	lodernd, tobend
raid	Plünderung
rapidly	schnell
ravenous	unbändig, unstillbar
raw	*hier:* wund
to recall	*hier:* erinnern an
to regain consciousness	wieder zu Bewusstsein kommen
to relieve	*hier:* abhelfen, mildern
remnant	Rest, Überbleibsel
remote	abgelegen
residence	Wohnhaus, Domizil
residential area	Wohngegend
resistant	widerstandsfähig, immun
to retrieve	finden, aufspüren
revelation	Enthüllung
revulsion	Ekel
to rip	(zer)reißen
to ripple	sich kräuseln, wogen
roar	Gebrüll

ruby	Rubin
rugged features *pl*	markante Gesichtszüge
to run riot	verrücktspielen
rush	Ansturm, Rausch
to sag	nachgeben, schlaff werden
sales policy	Verkaufsstrategie
scarlet	scharlachrot
scorching	*hier:* beißend
scoundrel	Halunke, Schurke (veraltet)
screeching	(Bremsen-)Quietschen
to screw	schrauben
to scurry	huschen
searing	schneidend, brennend
seduction	Verführung
sensation	Gefühl, Empfindung
to sense	spüren, wahrnehmen
sensually	sinnlich
shaken	erschüttert, aufgewühlt
to shed light on sth.	Aufschluss geben über etw.
to shroud	einhüllen
to shudder	schaudern, frösteln
sickening	entsetzlich
singed	angesengt, verbrannt
Slavic	slawisch
slender	schlank
sliver	Scheibchen; Schimmer, Strahl
sluggish	schleppend, träge
to slump	sinken, zusammensacken
smooth	glatt, weich
to snap	*hier:* blaffen
to snarl	wütend knurren
to snore	schnarchen
soberly	nüchtern, vernünftig
solitary	einzeln
solitude	Einsamkeit
spectator	Zuschauer(in)

spike	Spitze
to spit (spat, spat)	*hier:* fauchen
to splatter	(be)spritzen
to squawk	quäken
to squint	die Augen zusammenkneifen
stab	Anflug, Stich
stack	Stapel
stake	Pflock
to stake	aufspießen, pfählen
startling	erschreckend, verblüffend
stern	streng, hart
to stiffen	sich versteifen
to sting (stung, stung)	brennen, stechen
to stir	hervorrufen, erregen
to strain	(sich) spannen, anstrengen
to stumble	stolpern
stunted	*hier:* knorrig
substitute	Ersatz
supplies *pl*	Vorräte, Material
to support oneself	*hier:* sich auf den Beinen halten
to suppress sth.	etw. verdrängen
suspiciously	misstrauisch
to sympathize	Mitleid haben, mitfühlen
target	Ziel
to taunt	spotten, höhnen
taut	angespannt
tear	*hier:* Riss
to tear (tore, torn) away	losreißen
to tease	necken
telesales	Telefonmarketing
tentative	zaghaft, zögerlich
the hows and whys	das Wie und Warum
thigh	Oberschenkel
thrill	Kick, Erregung
thud	dumpfer Schlag
tickle	Kitzel
tight-knit community	enge Gemeinschaft

to toss and turn	sich hin und her wälzen
traitor	Verräter(in)
to trap	in eine Falle locken, fangen
to trigger sth.	etw. wecken, auslösen
tucked away	versteckt
twisted	verzerrt
unbearable	unerträglich
uncomprehendingly	verständnislos
undercurrent	Unterton
unearthly	überirdisch, unheimlich
unflinching	unbeirrbar, entschlossen
to unfold	enthüllt werden
unobtrusive	unauffällig
unsettling	beunruhigend
unspent	*hier:* anhaltend
viciously	*hier:* heftig
vivid	lebhaft, lebendig
vulnerably	verletzbar, prekär
vulture	Geier
to waft	wehen
to wager	wetten (veraltet)
waking memory	bewusste Erinnerung
ward	Station (Krankenhaus)
warehouse	Lagerhalle
to wash over sb.	jmd. überkommen
waver	Zögern, Schwanken
to whine	jammern, quengeln
whirlpool	Wirbel, Strudel
to wipe	*hier:* (aus)löschen
withered	vertrocknet
workhouse	Armenhaus
to wrinkle	(sich) runzeln
to writhe in unison	sich gemeinsam winden

Verzeichnis der Übungen

Abschlusstest

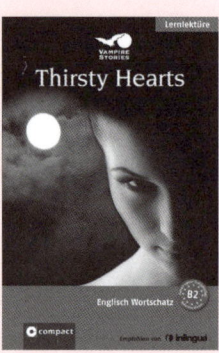
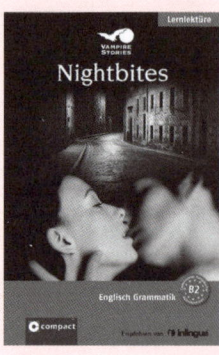